8 FIGURE
Exit Strategy

For HVAC
&
Plumbing Contractors

How To Grow Your
Contracting Business
Into An 8 Figure Empire
In As Little As 24 Months

Mike Layton &
Walter Bergeron
#1 Bestselling Author

8 Figure
Exit Strategy

For HVAC and Plumbing Contractors

How To Grow Your Contracting Business Into An 8 Figure Empire In As Little As 24 Months

By Walter Bergeron
& Mike Layton

Elite
Entrepreneur
Publishing

8 Figure Exit Strategy For HVAC and Plumbing Contractors

ISBN-13: 978-1516817405
ISBN-10: 1516817400

Published by Elite Entrepreneur Publishing

Visit the Author Website:
www.WalterBergeron.com
www.StochasticMkt.com

Disclaimer

About The Authors

Walter Bergeron is a down to earth, blue-collar, multi-millionaire serial entrepreneur owning and operating as many as six companies simultaneously. Mr. Bergeron is a best selling author and Marketer of the Year. This US Navy veteran started his entrepreneurial journey at the young age of 12, detailing automobiles in his parents' driveway. In 1996, after he completed a U.S. Navy tour aboard the nuclear powered aircraft carrier USS Carl Vinson, he started his industrial repair company in a small shed in the middle of the sugarcane fields of Louisiana. His entrepreneurial path has led him to the latest sale of one of his company's for $10 Million. He is now guiding other driven blue-collar entrepreneurs on a path to exponentially grow and sell their business to achieve their own eight figure lifestyle liberating payday.

Mike Layton is the son of an HVAC repairman who wanted his first born to go to college instead of turning wrenches for a living. After paying for college working summers as a pipe fitter (lots of wrenches) he went on to start, purchase or sell seven businesses (that all made money). After a founder of one of the nations largest, national HVAC and plumbing contracting groups asked him how to make contractor marketing more effective he came full circle, back to HVAC & plumbing. Using data analytics (putting all that college to work) his company Stochastic Marketing helps make hundreds of contractor's advertising more cost effective by identifying the prospects who are 600 X more likely to turn into a customer for an individual contractor. He is now working with Walter to help contractors build their businesses through acquisitions in the parts of their market where growth through marketing is ineffective.

Contents

Contents

Introduction

Life Altering Course Change

Welcome to what I sincerely desire to be a life altering course change in the direction you are heading with your entrepreneurial life. This book will reveal to the driven blue-collar entrepreneur, truths and secrets previously only available to mega sized corporations. The truths to be revealed will show you how to organically and exponentially grow your business simply by signing on the dotted line. The formula I reveal to you will show you the path to sell your business to get you your long deserved freedom. Time freedom, money freedom, freedom to live life on your terms and most importantly freedom earned early enough in your life to have many, many years to enjoy the fruits of your labor.

My Dad always said you should be able to do business with "A handshake and a man's good word." That's probably a pretty simplistic approach to business and a bit naïve, but it's pretty much how I started all of my companies. Well, a handshake a man's good word and of course my truck and toolbox were there too. I can't say my Dad was a very business savvy entrepreneur, his one venture into entrepreneurship failed miserably and he lost the business, his house and a huge chunk of his self-confidence.

I really wish I had been there at the end of his business to help him along the way, but I was in the bowels of an aircraft carrier in the middle of the Persian Gulf during a war in the early 90's. While he was liquidating all of his business and personal assets to pay off his debts, I was getting a blue-collar education from Uncle Sam. As my Dad's business was going under I was learning a trade, I was learning how to fix electronic equipment for nuclear power plants, a skill that would serve me for decades beyond my six-year enlistment in the US Navy.

My Dad was actually much happier and at peace after he lost his business, he always said he wasn't an entrepreneur and he inherited the problems of that business through an accidental family investment. I, on the other hand, grew up seeing his business through the eyes of a child. And I loved what I saw.

I began my entrepreneurial activities early on. At age 12, I was selling my car washing skills to every neighbor and friend of the family. By 16, I made my own "pay to play" board game and while in the US Navy I sold military equipment to my fellow sailors and soldiers to earn a few extra bucks, since the pay for a young enlisted sailor is quite minimal.

Living through the good and the bad of my Dad's entrepreneurial experiences I learned two very valuable lessons.

1. Entrepreneurship is an amazingly fun way to make a living and I will do it till the day I die. I love everything about it. I love being able to turn my ideas and my trade skills into a place that employed dozens and dozens of people and become a home to me and my wife and son. What a way to live!

2. I was never going to be at peace if my business ever failed, I would keep going until it provided me with a vast retirement income. I was certainly not going to end up like my Dad did, broke and starting all over again at almost 60 years old. Hoping social security was going to help him make it through his retirement in a few short years.

My business was going to be my retirement.
My Dad taught me a lot about money, savings and retirement. He always wanted me to build wealth and not just live like he chose to, in this paycheck-to-paycheck world. I always knew though, that the bulk of my personal retirement was going to be my business and I would always have an income since I owned the company. What I didn't take into account was that the world was going to change and my business may not be worth enough for me to retire at an age where I could sit back and rest for a while and enjoy a more relaxed, freer lifestyle.

If you listen to many "experts" you'll begin to hear the rumblings of things like "There are too many businesses going up for sale so this is going to drive down the price of your business". You may also hear about an economic "winter" that will be upon us in the next few years and businesses are going to suffer lower sales and poorer performance. Well, I must challenge these experts and tell you that you control your own destiny and that these so-called "problems" are simply opportunities for you to take advantage of. It's been said by so many billionaires that when times get rough, they get richer. That's because things are going up for sale at tremendous discounts and you simply have to shift your way of thinking to take full advantage of the changes in the business environment.

So, it is really awesome to be you right now. There is an amazing opportunity to be in your shoes at this very moment. Six-figure companies are in the "sweet spot" of opportunity for exponential business growth right now because so many entrepreneurs have gone before you and done what you want to do and been where you want to be. You no longer have to blaze the trail, you simply have to follow it! When I started doing this there was nothing like this available to me, no one had ever so concisely laid out the plan for me in a way that this book does. I would have crawled over hot coals on my hands and knees to get access to this level of wisdom. You get to learn from my mistakes and benefit from every bump and bruise I got along the way.

The path is fairly simple and straight-forward, so let me tell you where we are headed. First things first, I am going to show you how to use proven direct marketing to launch your organic growth and skyrocket your sales. Secondly, I'll explain how you are going to use technology to systematize the business, get it running on autopilot to prepare it for all of the upcoming growth you are getting ready to experience. Next, I'll reveal how to strategically acquire other businesses now, since the selection is high and you'll take advantage of the glut of baby-boomer businesses going up for sale. Turn what would seem to be a negative into a tremendous advantage for positive for you. This will enable you to grow your business to a value that is 500% larger than where you are now. Lastly, you are going to have built the business for a buyer that will pay you a premium so you can sell it to him and have the ability to live your truly liberated life from now on.

How to read this book

So if you ever want to sell your business in this current business environment then I urge you, for the sake of your family, to keep reading. I am going to show you a proven path to exponential growth and how to achieve a lifestyle of financial freedom and time freedom so that you can live the lifestyle you always dreamed that your business could provide to you and your family.

You've taken the first steps toward learning a life-changing model for exponential growth for your business. This book is your road map, along the way I'll show you what you need to do and when you need to do it. Along the way there'll be brainstorming sessions, worksheets and lots of planning and implementation. Mark the pages, crease the corners, highlight the pages and passages most relevant to your business and use this book as an invaluable weapon in your business arsenal. It's crucial to know each chapter in detail but more importantly you need to know how to gather a team behind you to support you in your efforts as well as help you when you need deeper, more penetrating knowledge and experience as you grow your business to the eight figure level.

Additional Resources

You've already taken the first step toward growing your six-figure business into a $10 million empire in as little as 24 months by reading this book. Are you ready to take the second step?

Are you ready to take the next logical step? Schedule your contractor market assessment. So you can identify the prospects that are 600 X more likely to turn into a new customer…and it's FREE too!

Simply go to www. MEERScore.com/freeoffer and fill out the application for a 45 minute phone call with Mike Layton.

As a special bonus, this includes an additional FREE strategy session to get your customized plan for exponential growth with Walter Bergeron.

Chapter 1

My Business Will Be My Retirement

Entrepreneurs Are Not Prepared

According to a survey conducted by American Express 60% of small business owners, entrepreneurs like you and me, say that they're not on track to save the money they need for retirement. And 73% said that they are legitimately worried that they won't have enough money saved to live the lifestyle they want, the lifestyle they deserve after they retire. And according to a 2012 study by the SBA, small business owners expect to have to work longer than their employees; they don't expect to retire until they are 72 years old while their own employees plan to retire years earlier. The simple conclusion is that most entrepreneurs are not prepared and not able to live the retirement lifestyle they deserve using conventional retirement methods like 401(k) plans, IRA's and investment portfolios. Quite simply, they will outlive their money.

Their Business Will Be Their Retirement

So how do many entrepreneurs intend to fund their retirement? You guessed it. Their business will serve as the financial means of retirement. Their plan is that when the time comes, they are going to sell the business and live off the proceeds. Or maybe the plan is to turn the business over to a trusted employee or family member and have them just continue to draw a salary to fund their retirement.

But there are many problems with this so-called plan. According to many economic experts including Harry Dent of Dent Research, there will be a glut of businesses for sale as well as an economic "winter" coming that will last for the next decade, which will substantially drive down the value of businesses that are for sale. That's if they can be sold at all.

To make matters worse, this economic winter is going to weaken many companies across just about every industry making them weaker and less profitable for their current owners.

Hope is your exit plan

Secondly, this isn't really a plan and that's why I've helped write this with Walter. It's more of a dream, because other than giving this thought some daydream time, there is no real defined path to get there. Certainly not an exact step-by-step set of instructions to get you from where you are right now at this exact moment to where you truly want to be in your life with your business sold or operating as a source of residual income. Your exit plan is at best just a rough idea in your head that "someday" you'll sell the business and "hopefully" that will secure the money you need for retirement. Well, we hate to be the bearers of bad news, but that's not a plan. That's just hoping things will work out. Hope is just a way to paint yourself into a corner and severely limit your exit options, especially if you wait until you <u>need</u> to sell the business because of many of life's unexpected challenges like health or financial needs.

Now hope is an interesting word because it's important to have hope if you need to hang on to something. Hope is a great word if you were stranded out at sea, waiting to be rescued. Hope is crucial if you are in a life-or-death situation and there are no other options available to you.

> In business, hope is an awful word. You never want to *hope* your business will grow…

But in business…hope is an awful word. You never want to hope that your business will grow. You never want to hope that the right buyer will come along and then hope that they'll offer you enough money for your business to fund your retirement. You never want to just hope your business will sell quickly when you do put it up for sale. And please don't rely on hope to make sure the business is worth enough to get you to the level of financial freedom you so strongly desire.

You will see this hope business strategy with business owners who never seem to get ahead. These are the HVAC or plumbing contractors who always seem to be struggling to find the next idea, the next shiny object that will set them free. But, nothing that they hope will work to help them get ahead with their businesses ever really does. They go it alone and never get to the level of growth they desire. These businesses just sort of fade away and go dark.

So we come back to the question again, are you just going to hope you can grow the business quickly? Are you just going to hope the business will be worth enough to retire? Are you just going to hope that the right buyer will come along and offer you enough money to never have a financial worry again? Or will you decide right now that this is not how you are going to plan your exit? Will you decide to choose to use a well-structured, well-thought-out, well-engineered, time-tested and proven plan? Are you going to choose a plan that will give you a surge of growth to quickly build your business to a level so that you get to choose how much excess money you have when you exit? You need to decide to either hope everything will work out or to plan your exit deliberately with a proven plan, a plan that includes growing the business by three, four, up to 10 times its current size.

The unprepared will suffer greatly

Thirdly, you are truly delusional if you think you're gonna' get top dollar for your business nowadays. You are in the "Baby Boomer Business Bubble" and there is currently a massive selloff of anywhere between 50% to as much as 75% of the roughly seven million privately held US companies with paid employees within the next 20 years. This large supply of businesses for sale is going to cause a glut in the market and will surely drive downward pressure on the pricing of businesses, especially for the unprepared entrepreneur.

This glut of businesses for sale is exacerbated by the tremendous lack of differentiation between these businesses. Many businesses are being operated as "me too" businesses. The widget-maker down the street looks just like your widget making company and just like the widget maker in any other town across the US. So how is any potential buyer to know what makes your business different and pay you a premium for your business? It is likely he is going to be able to pick and choose who he buys and your widget company will be picked clean by the time the dust settles and you retire.

This is only a part of the story. While the research is right, it is only referring to the businesses that make it to the selling point. There are many, many other business owners who just give up, those businesses that just quietly go dark because the owners have given up and quietly shut the lights off and gone home to live on their savings and Uncle Sam.

Research shows that 80% of penta-millionaires (those with a net worth of $5 million or more) are entrepreneurs who sold their businesses. Yep, that means that real wealth in not made by simply growing your business. Real wealth is made by selling your business. And particularly, selling it to someone who pays a premium for it because they believe they can generate more value, more money from what you've built. This is one of the best-kept-secrets. You have to show your buyer how they can build on top of what you've built and gain even more from your business than you could. You have to have a problem that they can solve immediately and gain tremendous value from that solution.

Your business is too small to be of interest to big deal makers who are set up and experienced in mergers and acquisitions. The guys that do this day in and day out with their own money for their own financial gain are not willing to waste their time on small fish with a sea full of gigantic catches worth over $50 million. So what is a small (<$10 million) business to do when they want to take the massive leap to selling their business? Who will be willing to guide the truly driven entrepreneur down the path to the sale and help them make it a payday large enough that they'll never have to work again another day in their lives? Well, the answer to that question lies within the pages of this book, so read on.

It's possible to do it all

It's not really your fault though. Up until this point in your business you have had to focus 100% of your time, energy, money and effort on growing, building and operating the company. So with all of this going on how can you be expected to plan the exit? You've known in the back of your mind that your exit plan is to sell it and you'll figure out how to get that done when you build the business "big enough".

Well, what if you were to discover through this very book in your hands right now that you can actually do both things at the same time? You can both grow the business as well as take massive steps towards selling it right now. Would that pique your interest? Growing your business and making preparations for selling it are not mutually exclusive activities. As a matter of a fact, they go hand-in-hand. They each help each other. Growth prepares the business to be sold for a higher price and sale preparation helps grow in the direction of your perfect buyer. You actually grow the business faster by preparing it for sale, especially when you develop a detailed plan with a definite time frame for completion.

The hidden secret behind the ultra-successful entrepreneurs is that they started thinking about selling or exiting the business early on. Specifically, they create an exit strategy, a plan that lays out the roadmap for them to grow their company when they start the business. They do this so they can exit for the maximum amount of money within a well-defined period of time and that is what you should do too.

> The hidden secret behind ultra-successful entrepreneurs is that they start thinking about selling their business early on.

We've watched contractors prep their company for sale by cutting back marketing or firing high cost employees to generate a short term boost to their bottom line, hoping that will boost their payout. That's a high-risk strategy if a sale doesn't go through. We've also seen HVAC and plumbing contractors grow to $10,000,000 in sales by buying the right small contractors located in complimentary parts of their market and harvesting replacement systems from new customers with better sales training.

There is a lot of good news here. The short-term success you need now to operate the business profitably and the long-term exponential growth you need to achieve your lifestyle of liberation are not mutually exclusive. You can accomplish both of these goals with the same plan. This plan is just more comprehensive and well thought out and engineered to give you a profitable and successful business now plus allow you to achieve the eight-figure exit you desire to live a lifestyle that you have always dreamed of.

Winners and Losers

The losers are just going to go dark. They are going to turn out the lights in exasperation because they never could find a buyer. That's about 50,000 small HVAC or plumbing contractors and after decades of being in business they didn't prepare themselves to sell the business to anyone. They put their heads in the sand and hoped maybe someday that someone would come along and offer them a great price for their business and that's when they would retire. Hope is not a plan.

The winners right now are the big guys. They are like rabid dogs licking their chops over all of the great sales going on. This is a tremendous going-out-of-business sale and it's your business that's going. But, they aren't looking for just any business to buy. With so many to choose from they can afford to be very picky and only the best and most prepared need apply for this game. The winners are taking advantage of the weaker, ignorant and lazy entrepreneur who refuses to prepare and make their business unique, to systematize it and learn the game of mergers and acquisitions so they can experience their rightfully earned day of liberation at a level that sets them up for the rest of their lives. You've got to commit to never letting your self-doubt stop you from having what you want, what you need, what you are driven to achieve.

Are you ready to take the next logical step? Schedule your contractor market assessment. So you can identify the prospects that are 600 X more likely to turn into a new customer…and it's FREE too!
Simply go to www. MEERScore.com/freeoffer and fill out the application for a 45 minute phone call with Mike Layton.

As a special bonus, this includes an additional FREE strategy session to get your customized plan for exponential growth with Walter Bergeron.

Chapter 2

How I Got Here

Let me share a quick story with you.

I have a picture on one of the shelves in my home library of my son. This family photo serves as a bittersweet reminder of the night I made the life-altering decision that I could not continue to go on working myself into an early grave because I didn't have a clear path for retirement, a clear exit plan from my business.

The picture was taken back in 2007. My wife Jana and I had been working yet another long weekend and we are having take-out pizza for dinner. This focal point of the picture is of my four year-old-son, smiling from ear to ear and just having a great time eating a slice of pizza while he sat at my workbench in the workshop at my industrial repair company. Imagine this, a four year old boy with pizza sauce smeared all over his face, as four year-olds will commonly have when eating anything. His white t-shirt is covered with red handprints, made compliments of the red marinara sauce and he's a genuine mess. But he's smiling ear to ear and having a great time because he gets to have dinner with Mom and Dad at work. Now he loved doing this, we did it pretty often and each time he sat at my workbench giggling and having a great time making his four-year old mess. But for me, from the other side of that camera, it was a completely different story.

This was the end of yet another full 20 plus hour weekend of work for us. Unfortunately, it was very common for my wife and I to be at work during meal times and we routinely had to order pizza because there was no time to do anything else for dinner. As I stood there taking this picture, a tremendous sense of dread took over me when I realized that this was never going to end. I had designed my business to work me to death through this vicious cycle and I didn't have a plan for it to ever end. We were going to be working 20 plus hours every single weekend and having to eat pizza every Sunday night at work until I was 80 years old. The path I was taking at that point was definitely the wrong path! It was that very night, at that very moment, that I decided to change the direction of my business so that it could provide me, and my little family a retirement.

What I have now is a job that I can never leave!

So, for the next 5 years I searched and searched for the solution to grow my business. I spent hundreds of thousands of dollars and a comparable number of man-hours searching for a solution. I hired dozens of experts and read hundreds of books and sifted through thousands of ideas. I tested, experimented and implemented just about all of them and eventually I discovered the optimal combination to achieve exponential growth.

The solutions I discovered are certainly not secret, as a matter of a fact the methods I tested and perfected for my business have been used by mega-corporations for over a century. I simply took these ultra powerful methods and condensed them and simplified them and made them affordable and reachable by the every-day, driven blue-collar entrepreneur.

> What I have now is a job that I can never leave.

Now some people may have concerns that this is all hype, that there is no way to grow a business this quickly and to this level especially if you are starting off with only six or maybe even seven figures in sales. There are many stubborn and closed-minded skeptics that don't think it's possible for an entrepreneur operating a $600k per year business to grow it to $10 million in 24 months from this very moment. I'll bet these are the same type of people that doubted business giants like Croc, Ford, Carnegie or Rockefeller. And just as these business giants proved their skeptics wrong, I would like to prove my skeptics wrong, because growing to eight figures in 24 months is exactly what I did.

Now I can assure you that you don't need any superhuman business abilities and you don't need to spend hundreds of thousands of dollars or even have a Ivy league MBA education to accomplish this feat. I did this with a blue collar industrial repair business that started out in the middle of the sugarcane fields in Louisiana and my education came from being an enlisted Navy sailor and a degree from a local college.

The feeble-minded skeptic might say that this can only be done in certain high growth industries or only in the "techy" types of companies, that it can't be done in your industry. Well, I have a client of mine that did it in a terribly commoditized and "non-techy", slow growth industry. He did it in the pest control industry. He's an exterminator and he got his business up to well over $10 million. But he did it the right way, which is what I am going to show you how to do right now.

I know what it's like to own a small struggling blue-collar business. I fully understand and have lived through hard times and failures and tremendous self-doubt. I don't have an ivy-league education, I didn't graduate from a highly academically accredited university. I was an enlisted US Navy sailor who learned my trade on an aircraft carrier during the first gulf war back in the early 90's. Then took that skill and started a company while living in a used mobile home, *a trailer*, between two sugarcane fields and started repairing televisions and VCR's in a small shed right next to my trailer. (Do you remember tube style televisions and tape VCR's)? Then, while that fragile little company was just getting started Hurricane Lily shred the roof off that little shed and it rained inside the building on all those electronics and nearly ruined that business. But, I was driven to make that company succeed. So me and my wife, who was four months pregnant, got up on top of the roof and nailed down one of those big blue tarps just to stop it from raining inside that building. So I know what it's like to get knocked down and beaten up and what it feels like when you've got that terrible feeling in your gut.

But with grit, determination, drive and then using the techniques I am going to deliver to you today, I took that little business and grew it. Then in 2012 I had grown it so well that it became the largest dedicated electronic repair facility in the entire country. The marketing and sales approach I used to grow it organically and exponentially earned me the title of Marketer Of The Year by the world's largest and most prestigious marketing training agency. And then, to top that off, I sold that little business for $10 million and I never have to work another day in my life. So I've run the gambit from teeny tiny little company in a shed to an eight-figure empire and I am no one special, if I can do it then you can certainly do it too. I met Mike Layton during our work with that marketing training agency. As I learned more about his experiences and his HVAC/plumbing data on acquisitions and their results, we decided we can help you do exactly what I did in your HVAC or plumbing business.

> If I can grow a company to the eight- figure level, then you certainly can do it too.

Can You Imagine

Sitting where you are today this may not seem like a very likely scenario. You may be one of those skeptics that doesn't believe that your business could possibly be positioned to be sold for eight figures, but I assure you that it can. It can be done by anyone that is truly focused and driven to achieve. I certainly won't lie to you and tell you that it will be easy or that you will be able to sit back and let someone else take the reigns and do this for you, that is not the case here. But with persistence and focus you can do this for yourself if you are a driven entrepreneur that want's to achieve a lifestyle of freedom that can only be attained by selling your business at this level.

There is a lot of work to be done, I should know, I did all of it myself. For the record, I am not an academic theorist on business. I don't sit at a desk and spout off my opinions about the theoretical operation, growth and sale of a business just by reading and studying about it. I have always used my own money, my own skills and knowledge and experience to start and grow my companies. I have made a lot of mistakes during the past 20 years and I am really excited for you right now because you get to learn from my mistakes and take the shortcuts that can only be seen from someone, like me, that has reached the destination you so vehemently want to reach.

Before we get into any of this, I want to let you know that none of what I am about to reveal to you should be considered advice on investing or legal advice or promises of any level of success. Business is a high-risk endeavor and this is all just food-for-thought and you should never, and I mean never, do any of this without the help of a properly qualified team of professionals consisting of at a minimum an experienced attorney and a CPA. These steps are to be used as possible strategies to propose to your team of professionals and then you as the business owner decide which path is best for you to take.

Are you ready to take the next logical step? Schedule your contractor market assessment. So you can identify the prospects that are 600 X more likely to turn into a new customer…and it's FREE too!
Simply go to www. MEERScore.com/freeoffer and fill out the application for a 45 minute phone call with Mike Layton.

As a special bonus, this includes an additional FREE strategy session to get your customized plan for exponential growth with Walter Bergeron.

Chapter 3

The
Framework

Follow the formula
MM + ROA + (OG x EG) + GOG = FREEDOM

Sure, it looks really complicated, until you get into the details of what it really means. The principles are solid, foundational business principles, though not always obvious to the blue-collar entrepreneur in the trenches of everyday business operations.

Marketing Makeover

The first phase of the 8 Figure Exit Formula™ process is about giving your business a Marketing Makeover. This makeover will make sure you have the foundational marketing systems in place and operating in your business, these are the foundational pieces that every type of business must have in place to achieve maximum growth potential such as website, newsletters, referrals, lost client reactivation, new client acquisition campaigns to name a few. Then you will need to implement the advanced marketing systems you need to have in place in your business to build your marketing system into a great asset. You will learn how to maximize marketing as a tremendous tool of leverage to be able to buy businesses at top dollar and still make that price a bargain. You will learn how to make your business valuation many multiples higher because you have made your marketing system into one of your greatest and most valuable assets. When I saw Stochastic's MEER Score report I knew that is MUST be part of the foundational marketing system for HVAC & plumbing contractors.

Running On Autopilot

The second phase of the 8 Figure Exit Formula™ process is called running on autopilot. In order for the business to run without your direct daily input and guidance, the major parts of the business must be documented and organized. More than a simple operations manual, the systems in your business must be able to provide initial and ongoing training for your staff. It must be able to be easily accessed and used in convenient as well as new and exciting ways. Development and documentation of these systems is not an academic exercise and must be proactively created with the input of your staff at the location where the system actions are being performed. The six major functions in your business that must at a minimum be fully documented are your Leadership, Management, Marketing, Sales, Money and Production Systems.

Growth On Steroids

The third phase of the 8 Figure Exit Formula™ process is growth on steroids and is designed to grow your company in multiples of up to five times it's current level. Growth at this level is accomplished by combining organic growth with acquisition growth. By giving you the tools to acquire other companies, this will allow your business to have growth in multiples much higher than organic growth alone could ever achieve in such a short time period. Acquiring other businesses can be the most viable alternative to grow your business rapidly and could ultimately be cheaper than organic business growth. It is the 'secret sauce' behind the bulking up of many mega corporations and can take place immediately in your business. You will discover the two essential elements of smart acquisitions and the most efficient ways to pay for your new company and then manage what you buy. Even if you decide not to close on a deal, you will enhance your ability to assess the strengths and weaknesses of your own organization as well as those you target to acquire and in the process you will get a rare opportunity to have a free look inside how other businesses run and what makes them successful. So pay close attention to the mega strategies being shared with you.

Get Out While The Getting's Good

The fourth phase of the 8 Figure Exit Formula™ process is getting out while the gettins' good. Now that the business is growing quickly, it's time to plan an exit strategy and prepare the business for your exit. It is now time for the plan of attack on your secession from the business. Audit of financials, stock sale versus asset sale and many other areas need to be addresses at this time. It is here that we entertain offers and accept letters of intent to buy your company. Then we close on your sale and you become free of the business to begin the process of enjoying your newfound liberated lifestyle.

Are you ready to take the next logical step? Schedule your contractor market assessment. So you can identify the prospects that are 600 X more likely to turn into a new customer…and it's FREE too!
Simply go to www. MEERScore.com/freeoffer and fill out the application for a 45 minute phone call with Mike Layton.

As a special bonus, this includes an additional FREE strategy session to get your customized plan for exponential growth with Walter Bergeron.

Chapter 4

Marketing Makeover

What has marketing got to do with it?

You may be wondering to yourself why is marketing needed for business buying and selling. You may be thinking that you want to learn how to exponentially grow through acquisitions and that marketing is simply a method to grow your business organically. But, you must know right now that marketing is an absolutely crucial component to exponential growth and that a marketing system is an asset that very few businesses have. This tremendously valuable asset can allow you to pay top dollar for a company and yet make that purchase a bargain. For most businesses, marketing tends to be done 'accidentally' with no real rhyme or reason as to why it's done or the outcome or result that it must achieve. It is so very common for businesses to fall victim to ad agencies or marketing firms that focus on building a company's brand and using marketing with platitudes. It's also very common that this type of marketing fails for the typical entrepreneur because they think that marketing like mega corporations is what they need to do to be successful. The fact is though, that without the marketing budget that these corporations have or without the room for errors that these large corporations have, marketing that is focused 100% on brand building, will bankrupt you in a heartbeat. So a different type of marketing is needed, it's called direct marketing. Direct marketing focuses on gaining new clients and keeping existing clients. Then, your brand is built as a happy and free by product of good direct marketing.

With a profitable direct marketing system in place, you will position yourself infinitely better to be able to purchase other companies that have poorly done marketing, or better yet, no marketing system at all. Then you can come in and put your system into place and make then new businesses you purchase become an instant success. You'll find businesses with terrible marketing and implement your system and more quickly reap greater profits because you have an instant solution to a problem with your new acquisition. This is one of the ways wealth is built into organic business growth like marketing, and then turned into exponential growth when combined with acquisitions.

Additionally, with a profitable and well-documented marketing system you also position yourself for a bigger payday when it comes time to sell the company that you've built into an empire. The buyer of your business will demand great systems to be in place, especially when you get to the eight figure level transactions, and you'll have a great system in place to sell to them. And because your system is well documented and proven to work time and time again you won't have to cater to lowball offers of 2 or 3 times earnings, you'll be able to entertain offers with 5, 6 or 7 times earnings offers and pick which one suits you best. When companies look to buy companies like yours, they will pay more for companies that have a great foundational marketing system.

So, all great direct marketing systems consist of 3 major parts. These 3 major parts combine to form what one of our mentors Mr. Dan S. Kennedy calls the Direct Marketing Results Triangle. Part #1 is the message, Part #2 is the market and Part #3 is the media. (See Figure 4.1)

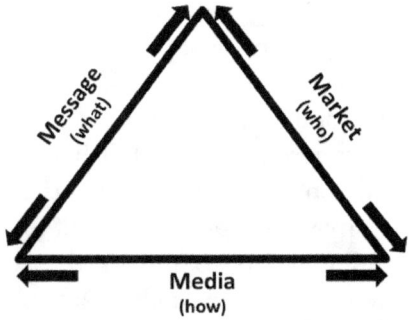

Figure 4.1

Market

In order to jump start your direct marketing system, there is an exercise that you will need to complete that will give you the first two parts of the direct marketing results triangle. This exercise will help you develop your market and your message at the same time by having you answer some in depth questions about your client.

This is also where I started. The foundation of my marketing system had to start here so nothing got missed and I could make sure I covered the message, the market and the media. The first step is to start with the market, start with your clients. I really thought I knew who my market was, after all I had been doing business with them for over a decade before I did this exercise. Granted, my company was a business-to-business company not business-to-consumer company like most residential HVAC or plumbing contractors. Because many HVAC or plumbing contractors have two sides to their business, the "commercial" or business-to-business side and the "residential" or business-to-consumer side they should consider approaching the "commercial" side of their marketing differently than they do the "residential" side.

Now this first one is a real "writer downer", it is extremely important because I fell victim to a "one size fits all" attitude. After doing this exercise I found out just how wrong I was. I discovered that I didn't have 1 type of client I had 4 distinct and separate types of clients. I also found out they are worth anywhere between $3800 to as much as $34,000, each and that led to me to the realization that I could spend more on one type of client and strategically focus my marketing efforts where they would have the biggest bang for the buck.

I used Department of labor for market size, I used survey monkey for demographics and psychographics, I dug really deep into our own internal CRM software for client spending details. I found out who my market was, no more guessing necessary! I then gave my 4 markets distinct names to identify them easily as well as reminded myself how much they add to the bottom line. These are the avatars so I could see who they were and become more connected with them as "commercial" clients.

The second result of this exercise will be determining your message and creating your unique selling proposition, your unique message to your clients. When I did this exercise it revealed to me that I couldn't create just one USP, I had to create multiple USP's for commercial customers, each one of them spoke to my different target audiences in a way that relates uniquely to them and gave me a greater affinity to that market.

So going forward you will need to go through the worksheets and find your target market and your message and USP before we move on to the next part of foundational marketing.

Step 1 is to determine who is your target market in complete detail. It is of utmost importance and the first step to being able to create a marketing system that will be effective. Then go on to create your commercial customer avatar. This process starts with questions about that market. You must answer them with as much accuracy as you possibly can and as thoroughly as possible. This means that it may take research in multiple areas and using many sources of this data. Below are some ideas on what to use to get started. Take a look at the form and fill it out to outline a plan to conduct the necessary research on the "commercial" side of your business:

Research:
- ❑ U.S. Department of Labor
- ❑ Surveys
- ❑ Magazine advertising departments
- ❑ Your own internal software systems and internal client records
- ❑ Ask your clients directly, call them, email them or face to face conversations

- *How does your target market talk to each other?*
- *What does a day in their life look like?*
- *Who has tried to sell to them and screwed it up?*
- *Do they have a special language that they speak or specific terms that they use that someone NOT in that market would make them stand out as an insider? A "residential" contractor who uses residential sales or service techniques to sell to "commercial" clients will struggle just like a "commercial" contractor will struggle in the residential market if he approaches homeowners the same way they sell to business owners.*
- *What are they afraid of?*
- *What are they angry about?*

- *Who are they angry at?*
- *What are their top 3 daily frustrations?*
- *What trends are occurring in their businesses or lives?*
- *What do they secretly, privately desire the most about your product or service?*
- *Is there a built in bias to the way they make decisions?*
- *Do you have a specific affinity to your client?*
- *What types of print media do they use?*
- *What other types of print media do they use?*
- *What associations, clubs or organizations do they belong to?*
- *Who else sells to your target market?*
- *Who are your direct competitors?*
- *What are the unmet needs of your client?*
- *What do you do better than your competitor?*
- *What keeps them awake at night?*
- *Does your target market divide up into sub cultures or sub niches?*

- *Are there any other key divisions that will enable you to market differently to groups of these markets?*
- *What is the size of your market?*
- *What is the rate of new entrants into your market?*

Photo

Truly identify and picture your "commercial" client. Some people call these avatars; I just want you to get a clear picture on paper of exactly who your client is. Find a picture that is an exact representation of your client.

Now handwrite a heartfelt letter to yourself from your client. Write a personal letter from your prospect to you, your prospect is going to describe the things above and describing how you can help them. With this method you become the character, you become your client and write a letter from them to you. Then read that letter out load to yourself and now whenever you create any of your marketing pieces you picture this person and you write directly to them. You are always writing to this person, all of your communication is directed to this person. Now all of your "commercial"

> Four Criteria for the BEST type of client, Your Hungry Buying Audience.
> 1. Insanely passionate
> 2. Large in numbers
> 3. Easy to reach
> 4. Someone you would actually not mind hanging around with

marketing will have a whole new depth to it and your client will feel like you truly understand them. Your business is all about building powerful relationships. You are now light years ahead of everyone else in your market. You can now make a great connection to your customers.

Questions You Should Be Asking To Get More Clients:
1) How Can I reach more of them tomorrow?

2) Who is already reaching them?
3) Who is selling them the most stuff?
4) What are they doing that I am not doing?
5) Who are the clients you actually have?
6) Who are the clients you think you have?
7) Who are the clients that you really, really want?

Getting Residential HVAC or Plumbing Clients

There is no shortage of information available on residential contractor marketing. If you are reading this chapter you have been exposed to lots of advise on ways to use the following to grow your residential HVAC or plumbing business:

Yellow Pages
Direct Mail
Search Engine Optimization
Branding efforts (wrapping your vans, radio vs television, etc.)
Home Shows
Newsletters
E-mail marketing
Blogging
Facebook, Twitter, Angie's List
Ad words vs Google Maps vs Mobile optimization
Pay-per-Click
Etc., etc.

You've also been told to use tracking numbers so you can track marketing ROI (we will get back to that later) to be sure that your marketing expense stays within some industry "benchmarks" like 6-8% to moderate growth, 10% for aggressive growth, etc..

Marketing companies selling direct mail, or radio or web services will point to the use of their service by a successful contractor as proof that:

Long term branding efforts via radio is the secret to growth

Mailing for service is the way to get new customers

The Internet is the cheapest way to get new customers

What these marketing pros don't seem to ask is "Is marketing success the cause of contractor success or just correlated with contractor success?"

Before you lay out your residential marketing plan and decide what you should be willing to spend to get a new customer, shouldn't you establish how much your client's are worth to you?

The investments you make in branding (for instance on radio spots) will in all likelihood result in more visits to your website, same for direct mail or wrapping your trucks. So even the most diligent use of call tracking won't give you a precise Return on Investment measurement in the short term (because several marketing investments interact to generate a lead).

Since about 40% of customer's value comes 1 or more years after your first visit to their home, marketing ROI calculation are either very difficult or impossible to calculate for residential HVAC or plumbing contractors.

If HVAC and plumbing contractors can't really determine their marketing ROI, how do they make sound marketing investments?

The good news is you can use the processes that other industries use when placing educated bets with their marketing dollars. The bad news is, this involves some math and statistics.

Think of it this way. If you wanted to catch a fish and you went to your local Bass Pro or Cabelas store (who are both very sophisticated, successful marketers) and said "I need to invest in some fishing equipment, because I'd like to catch my own fish" wouldn't you expect them ask what type of fish you wanted to catch? how many? where were you planning on fishing?

If you are just going to take your six year old grandson fishing for bluegill in your subdivision's pond, you probably expect to spend a lot less on fishing equipment than you would if you were taking his father deep sea fishing for Marlin.
Investing in contractor marketing is a lot like investing in fishing equipment (or a fishing guide).

The First Question For Residential Contractor Marketing (doing some simple math)

The first question you have to ask yourself as you build a marketing plan is "how much is a new customer worth to me"? This should be simple enough, software systems like Successware, ESC, Service Titans and even Quick Books collect billing information on every visit to a customer's home.

Sophisticated marketers like Cabelas or Bass Pro know the details of every recent (past 5-7 years) purchase, whether you bought on line, via their call center or at a retail store. They have a plan for moving you from buying the first fishing lure to the $25,000 bass boat.

Likewise, fundraisers for universities, politicians or organizations like the American Cancer Society understand that before they can expect a large donation they usually have to start with a small donation just $25 or $50 bucks. Their systems not only tell them how much it costs to get a new donor (and they will lose money on marketing to start the customer relationship) but how important it is to keep their "customers" buying.

They understand what an average new customer is worth in the first 30 days of the relationship, in the first year and over the lifetime of the relationship.

Sophisticated marketers hire outside marketing professionals or buy marketing services based on their understanding of their value of a new customer within 30 days of the first order, within 12 months of the first order and over the next 5-7 years.

If you are making marketing investments without this information, you aren't placing very smart bets.

Check your numbers before building your marketing plan

For residential HVAC or plumbing contractors, in any given year, 60-80% of your revenue will come from new customers. Allocate your marketing dollars accordingly. If you have been told that the key to building a successful contractor is growing your club list and maintaining a long-term relationship with customers, that's only half right. On average an existing customer is worth less than half as much as a new customer because 50% of the lifetime value of a residential HVAC or plumbing customer is captured within 30 days of the first visit to the home. We've looked at more than 25 MILLION contractor homes. These ratios show up over and over because that is why consumers call you, they have a problem and they want a solution, NOW. If your team (techs, plumbers or sales people) is in front of good prospects, and they are closing at good value added price levels, a new customer is worth almost 4 times as much as an existing customer.

An average new HVAC customer should be worth approximately $2000 - $2500 during the first year of their relationship with the contractor. If the Pay per click, SEO, Yellow Pages, etc. is bringing in customers worth less than this, these forms of advertising may actually be reducing the value of your business if the aren't producing new customers at _very_ low costs.

In fairness to your marketing suppliers, they may legitimately offer advice based on their success with one of their customers. You may check out their references web sites, listen to their radio spots or watch samples of their cable TV ads. It's very likely that they are offering good advice, based on their experience.

But if you follow advice based on correlation, not causation (the marketing results they brag about are great because their contractor gets $2600 from their average new customer) you may be very disappointed if you don't know the size of the fish you typically catch (if your average new customer is typically worth $1300 your marketing has to work twice as well to get the same revenue).

You can't fish everywhere (or using statistics as your fish finder)

Years ago, Ron Smith pointed out that you should divide your market into primary areas, secondary areas and don't go there areas. It turns out, he was right. He may not have known why he was right, but the mathematical principle behind his insight was the Pareto distribution, commonly called the 80/20 rule or the Bell Curve.

A typical HVAC contractor with $2,500,000 - $3,000,000 in sales in a metropolitan area may find himself doing business in up to ninety zip codes. Each of those zip codes will usually have ten to fifteen thousand households. Radio, television, newspaper, Internet advertising may expose you to 90,000 households over the course of year. The typical contractor this size will sell more than $100,000 per year in only 8 – 10 out of 90 zip codes that are exposed to their advertising. These zip codes should be the main focus of all your marketing or advertising because prospects in those 8 – 10 zip codes are 600 times more likely to turn into your customer than identical prospects, exposed to the same weather serviced by the same techs or plumbers as the other 80 zip codes that your vans travel to, occasionally.

After reviewing nearly twenty five million contractor customer records, statistically, just as the Pareto distribution or the 80/20 rule predicted, more than 70% of the typical contractor's new customers will be found in around ten out of ninety zip codes. Half of your marketing dollars will fall on areas where you have almost NO chance of gaining new customers. In fact, in the zip codes where you sell more than $100,000 per year you are 600 X more likely to generate a new, valuable customer than the next 34 zip codes that a typical contractor usually sells between $100,000 and $10,000 per year. Normally a $2,500,000 - $3,000,000 contractor will send his techs or plumbers to an additional 45-48 zip codes where the contractor sells less than $10,000 per year.

Advertising that falls on these zip codes is usually more 1000 times LESS likely to generate a new customer than the contractor's top 8 – 10 zip codes.

When you look at your residential market, advertising in more than half of it generates almost NO new customers. In this part of your market, your advertising actually drives business to your competitors. Likewise, advertising by your competitors in your top 8 – 10 zip codes is more likely to drive new customers to you than it is to create new customers for them.

So the challenging question for any residential HVAC or plumbing contractor is where should you invest your marketing dollars if you want organic growth? The most cost effective way to generate organic growth is by growing your business in areas where it is already strong. In the 50% of your market area where organic growth via advertising is very expensive, growth through acquisition may be a faster, less expensive way to find the 100 – 150 new customers per year per zip code that you need to establish in order to support cost effective organic growth.

That's why we wrote this book, to give HVAC or plumbing contractors a blue print for building wealth in residential or light commercial businesses with a mix of organic growth through better marketing and strategic acquisitions.

Building a Profile of Your "Commercial Clients"

Example: Once I got everything written down by hand I put it into a word document and then kept adding to it as I found out more detailed information about my clients. (See Figures 4.2 and 4.3)

For our General Industrial Electronic Repair service			
END USERS - Manufacturers – NAICS Codes 31, 32 and 33 - 332,536 Establishments - 13,395,670 Employees			
Establishments in the Manufacturing sector are often described as plants, factories, or mills and characteristically use power-driven machines and materials-handling equipment. However, establishments that transform materials or substances into new products by hand or in the worker's home and those engaged in selling to the general public products made on the same premises from which they are sold, such as bakeries, candy stores, and custom tailors, may also be included in this sector. Manufacturing establishments may process materials or may contract with other establishments to process their materials for them. Both types of establishments are included in manufacturing.			
49-1011	First Line Supervisors of Mechanics, Installers and Repairers *Directly supervise and coordinate the activities of mechanics, installers, and repairers. Excludes team or work leaders.*	49,470	$65,420
49-2094	Electrical and Electronics Repairers, Commercial and Industrial Equipment *Repair, test, adjust, or install electronic equipment, such as industrial controls, transmitters, and antennas.*	21,570	$51,340
49-9041	Industrial Machinery Mechanics *Repair, install, adjust, or maintain industrial production and processing machinery or refinery and pipeline distribution systems.*	157,760	$46,910
11-3061	Purchasing Managers *Plan, direct, or coordinate the activities of buyers, purchasing officers, and related workers involved in purchasing materials, products, and services. Includes wholesale or retail trade merchandising managers and procurement managers.*	23,050	$94,630
13-1023	Purchasing Agents, Except Wholesale, Retail and Farm Products *Purchase machinery, equipment, tools, parts, supplies, or services necessary for the operation of an establishment.*	91,790	$57,680
	Total High Probability Prospects	*343,640*	
More Questions:			
What keeps them awake at night?			
Production line shut down due to equipment breakdown, losing tons of money every hour production is not at 100%			
What are they afraid of?			
Loss of production			
What are they angry about?			
Equipment not lasting and failing in the middle of the night every time it fails			
Who are they angry at?			
Vendors that supplied them equipment or vendors that cannot meet their time demands to get production back up quickly			
What are their top three daily frustrations?			
1. Broken equipment that they are at some else's mercy to get up and running again 2. Dealing with middle management demands like meetings 3. Paperwork – they would rather just do the hands on work and avoid the paperwork			
What trends are occurring and will occur in their businesses or lives?			
Manufacturing jobs are sacred, they don't want to lose their good paying jobs so they are loyal company men			
What do they secretly, ardently desire most?			
To be known as super hard working blue collar men that are the solution when things go wrong and they look like the hero in their bosses eyes.			
Is there a built in bias to the way they make decisions?			
Impatient and cost sensitive			
Do they have their own language?			
Industrial equipment has special names that they use such as VFD's and HMI's they like mneumonics and abbreviations so they sound technical and can keep laymen out of the conversation and they sound smart.			
Print Media		**Other Media**	
Maintenance Technology Magazine Plant Engineering and Maintenance Magazine Industrial Maintenance and Plant Operations (IMPO) Magazine Reliable Plant Magazine Control Engineering		All print media have websites as well as print publications Globalspec.com Manufacturing.net	

Figure 4.2

Plant Services Magazine Chief Engineer Magazine Uptime Magazine Manufacturing Engineering Magazine NASA Tech Briefs Maintenance world	
Associations, clubs, organizations	**Mailing Lists**
IEEE International Facility Management Association Institute of Industrial Engineers International Standards Organization NEMA	Lists from the print media and organizations they subscribe to are easy to buy or rent Their job description list can be purchased from many list services
Where do they gather?	**Market Influencers for Joint Ventures**
Routine company meetings for their departments Tradeshows Distributor Open Houses	Distributors is who we currently use in just this role, so we will use them for their national accounts that have already been set up. Applied Industrial Technologies, Motion Industries, Kaman – national distributors Missouri Power, Ralph's, IES – Regional distributors These distributors are from all types of specialties and don't necessarily have to have anything to do with electronics to sell these services, they just have to have industrial OEM clients they serve.
Responsiveness	**Affordable Reachability**
They already have a relationship with local distributor vendors and trust what they sell, they respond very well to these salesmen and use whatever services they provide due to the personal relationship and convenience of one single vendor providing multiple services. Direct marketing to them is not as well received, there is a lot of apprehension if our services are unknown to them but this can be overcome with frequent repeated information and then referral from colleagues	Purchasing the job function lists from the magazine publishers and then conducting direct mail and email campaigns would be the most affordable and highest scale. The low scale and very cheap method would be cold calls to the list but better to support that with direct mail and email pieces anyway. Possibly a combination of mail, email and calls would work best. Partnering with distributors to sell our services
Who else sells to this market?	**Direct Competitors**
Online – all of our competitors sell with SEO, online pricing – none of them use any type of lead capture very well maybe only one of them uses free reports to capture leads Offline – Almost none of them use direct marketing at all much less in sequential steps They use some cold calling techniques and outside sales forces	**PLC Center** USP: Quality Brands Competitive Prices One Source For: -MRO -Welding -Pipe Line -Construction The largest in the industry but they sell new as well as repairs. $50M – 1/3 of that overseas but not sure how much repairs versus new they do. **Electrical South** USP: Repair Support for over 100,000 part numbers Full functional testing to provide the best repair quality Cost effective, quality alternatives to buying new 70,000 sf facility – providing the best repairs Repair history, repair order status and quote approvals on-line 24/7 The largest in the industry but they sell new as well as repairs. $50M – 1/3 of that overseas but not sure how much repairs versus new they do.

Here are my examples of my clients. I thought I only

Figure 4.3

had 1 type of client and I discovered that I actually had 4. I used clipart and found pictures that made these people more real to me. I then put some of the major facts about them so I could be constantly reminded of what they mean to my business. (See Figure 4.4)

 Outside Salesman – *Sam Sellers*
$34,575.95 – 22.46 Months

 Maintenance Manager – *Mike Hammer*
$3882.47 – 6.99 Months

 Tyson Foods Manager – *Chuck Poultry*
$25537.63 – 21.91Months

 Platinum Member – *Phil Medal*
$34,575 – 22 Months

Figure 4.4

Message

Now, with all of your research completed you can create your message, your unique selling proposition for either commercial or residential. The best businesses, the most successful ones, have a message that stands out and sets them apart from everyone else. Their message will answer the following question better than everyone else in their market. The question is this:

Why would my client do business with me versus any other option available to them, including doing nothing at all?

The answer to this question gives you a clear message to communicate to your clients and without it there is no need to move forward with the media because you don't know what to say in the media. So take some time and get this right, right now and it will make life much, much easier for you.

As you complete this exercise, I am sure what you will find is that your competitors will probably start to all have very similar messages, very similar promises, very similar deliverables. If you find this true, compare your message to every one else's and see if yours is drowning in this sea of sameness and banality. If you find that your message is the same, what do you think your potential new clients are thinking? What message do you think they are getting from you? Is it the same old message as everyone else or is yours unique, is it different, does it stand out? If it doesn't, then not only is your product or service a simple commodity, but you are describing it with trite platitudes and making it look just like everyone else does. This is a great formula to make sure you struggle to grow your business, a great plan to have the same level growth as everyone else. In the residential HVAC or plumbing business where your have literally hundreds of local competitors selling basically the same products or services about the only way to make yourself stand out by is being one of the most active contractors in a <u>very</u> small part of your market (8 or 10 zip codes). Even then, less than 1% of the homeowners in your best zip codes will do business with you in a given year.

If you don't have a compelling answer to this question then you do not have a message worth hearing, your message is trite and biased even if you deliver it as if it were significant and original. Your message is simply a platitude.

Counterintuitive messages

Take a counterintuitive approach to make your message stand out. They have heard the same message many times from everyone else, so to make yours stand out make it counterintuitive. Think of other approaches to the same product or service that others have not thought of. Bring attention to applications of your product not thought of by others or just not a message delivered by you competitors. The reason to do this is that the first thing prospects do when they hear a message, since they hear so many messages, is that they try to disqualify themselves from your product or service.

How to get to the uniqueness of your message

The process of getting to your message, a message that resonates with your market is done in two parts. Part one is to develop your unique selling proposition. This is your promise to your client that doing business with you is their best option, it's even better to do business with you than to do nothing at all. To get the USP correct can take many, many revisions, but with the following exercise you will have the details of who your client is and the pain and frustrations they are are experiencing. Use that information to develop the second part of your message and that is a story that builds an affinity between you and your commercial clients.

- ➤ **The USP exercise for commercial or residential contractors:**
- ➤ How sensitive is your market to pricing?
- ➤ How passionate is your market about what they do and the solutions you may provide?
- ➤ Where is there an opportunity for you to position yourself within this market?
- ➤ Who else has tried to sell something to this market that is similar, how has it failed?
- ➤ What is your story of why you are a part of this market?
- ➤ Do you have a low point in your career?
- ➤ What is your high point in your career?
- ➤ Do you have any pictures that remind you of the story?
- ➤ Now that you have some details, the following question will bring you your USP.

Your USP should ideally have 3 parts to it.

- ➤ It should have a narrowly defined position – you can't be everything to everyone and commercial clients are very different than residential clients
- ➤ It must have meaningful specifics - these are the direct benefits to your client
- ➤ Ideally it should have a guarantee – you can always find something to guarantee

Why should your client do business with you instead of any other option available to them?

The second part to your message is a story. The story is also critical to forming a better bond between you and your client so don't take this for granted. The story must serve to entertain your clients and give you a tighter affinity to them. Your relationship with your market must have entertainment and not just education. Johnny Carson was once interviewed and he had a great comment to the interviewer. Johnny said to compare the salary of him versus the salary of the Dean of Harvard and then tell him what America values more, entertainment or education. Your story is important and it must entertain. Now, take your answers and tell your client a compelling story. Start with why you entered the market, then move to your low point that caused you a great deal of pain. Then move to your success and lead into your passion for this industry and how it relates to your client. Add examples of any transitions you made in your journey. Wrap that all up and you have the foundation to your story. An advanced version of your story can be tailor made to the audience. When my company was selling our services to defense contractors I always focused on the part of my story that dealt with being member of the US Navy and now being a proud veteran. But that message never resonated with my Japanese auto-manufacturing clients. So I would use another part of my story with them that dealt with quality and sacrifice. You can do this as well by tailoring what you say to what type of audience you are trying to attract to you.

Media

The media we use will be highly focused and dependent on which one of the types of clients we are trying to reach. So now let me introduce you to the Direct Marketing Client Lifecycle. This is the typical lifecycle that each type of client you have goes through during a transaction with your business. Your 4 types of clients are Existing Clients, Referral Clients, Lost Clients and New Clients. Your best and easiest type of client to sell to will be your existing clients, whether they are commercial or residential customers. You already have all of their contact information and an established relationship. You know how they operate and they know how you operate. There is already a high level of trust and now you must develop new messages as well as products and services to keep them as a part of your herd. The foundational types of media we are going to use to communicate with them include the website, newsletters and campaigns. Referred clients are the next best and easiest type of client to sell to. They will come to you with an existing level of trust depending on the relationship they have with whomever referred them to you and with whatever message you put in place through your referral generation process.

We'll use a well planned out referral program to make sure we have a steady flow of referrals to your business. Your third best clients are your lost clients. These are clients that have bought from you in the past but have not done a recent purchase with you. You will need to determine how long before you consider them as lost clients. You will also need to overcome why they left you in the first place, but much research has been done to find that in many cases the reason is that you ignored them in some way. Make them feel special again and win them back.

Your most difficult market to reach are your new clients, but many entrepreneurs focus so much effort on this area. Don't underestimate the time and resources it will take to find out how to deliver a message to this market, what the message must say and the types and volume of media to communicate with them. This type of client will take far more money and time to convert to a sale than the other 3 types of clients.

It is very likely that you will not just have one type of client, you will have many market segments of each type of client particularly if you are doing light commercial HVAC or plumbing along with residential. You will need to communicate with each of them with a different message and in some cases with different media. So not only will you have existing, referral, lost and new clients, but you will develop different messages for each of these market segments. (See Figure 4.5)

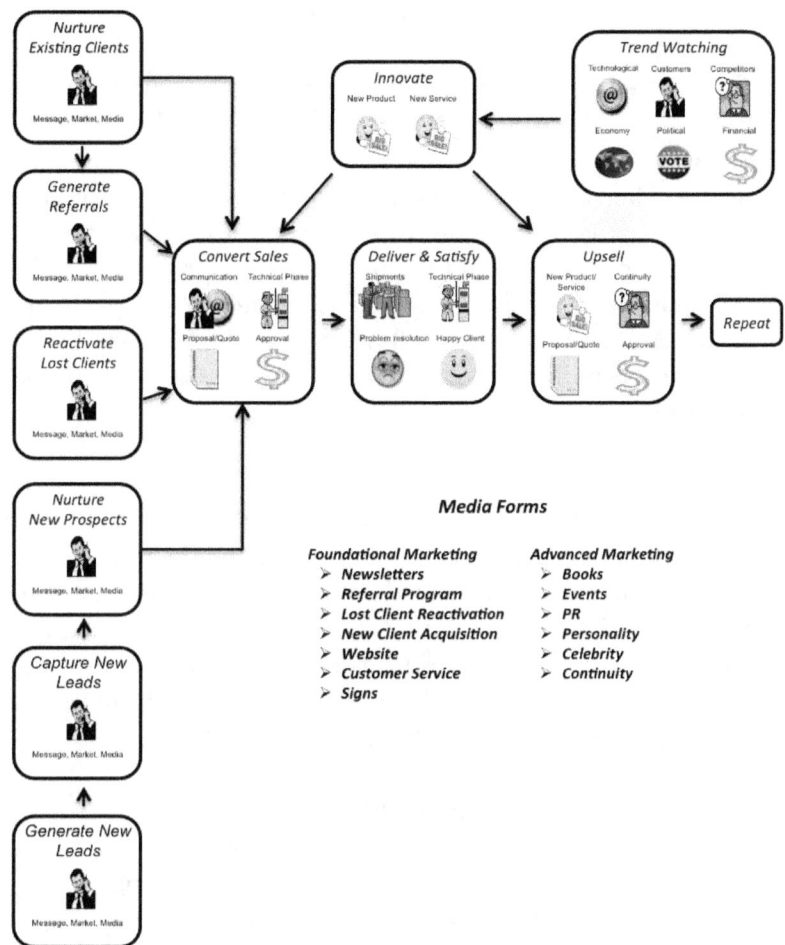

Figure 4.5

Newsletters

Newsletters are the backbone to maintaining a fence around your herd of commercial customers. Newsletters are the way you maintain relationships with your commercial clients. They are like sitting down to have a hot cup of coffee with a friend and actually this is how they are written, as a conversation piece, not an education piece or a sales pitch. It will take form in printed as well as online formats to achieve maximum exposure as well as it will have a customized message enabling you to reach each major category of client you have.

The Structure

Your conversations have structure, just like you're your newsletters will have structure. When you sit down with a friend the first thing you do is catch up with what you've been up to. Then you chat a little about current events, a few fun facts or trivia, touch on business and then wrap it up by saying you'll stay in touch and what you'll talk about next time. This is the structure the newsletter will have too.

Segmentation

Now, when it comes to conversations you typically change the context a little to fit who you are talking to. If you are speaking to a friend from work, your friendly conversation will steer away from work topics to keep the conversation more interesting. Conversely in a conversation with a friend from your neighborhood, you might find the work topic captivating and interesting conversation. So, in the previous section when you determined that you have more than one type of client, you can now segment your list and customize your newsletter for each different commercial market segment.

Changing only a section or two in the newsletter makes it a more suitable and a more specific conversation piece for each type of client instead of a generic, one size fits all, boring newsletter. Keep it entertaining and interesting to each type of client.

In my industrial repair business I found out when I did my market research that I had four types of clients so I also had four newsletters that I created each and every month. Now, before you think that having four newsletters is crazy and way too much work to do, I took shortcuts. I had the same template each month for the newsletters and I simply changed one or two articles within the newsletter to customize it to my audience. They were not four completely different types of newsletters, they were basically the same newsletter tweaked to suit the tastes and needs of each audience.

Client Value

You must physically mail a printed newsletter to your commercial clients. Don't be cheap on this. That four-page newsletter that I just outlined costs just over a dollar to mail. So if you have clients that aren't even worth $12 a year, then maybe you should examine your client list first and not jump to condemning your newsletter practices. The average lifetime value of a "light commercial" client is often $25,000 - $35,000 vs an average lifetime residential customer value of $2,500. Newsletters may not be the best approach for residential customers.

Distribution

Not only do you want to send a physical printed newsletter, but you want to repurpose it and use it in every other place that you interact with your commercial clients. My clients would receive a physical printed copy of the newsletter monthly as well as on a weekly basis they would receive a portion of the newsletter electronically too. In my industrial repair business we actually received equipment from our clients, so we eventually shipped equipment back to them. This meant that they were receiving boxes and packages from us routinely and inside every single one of those boxes we would put another printed copy the newsletter. We would also make sure that anyone in the office or shipping receiving department or any inside sales staff would give out a copy of our newsletter when clients dropped by the office. This means that by creating the content once you can deliver it in five different ways. In my business that meant that since we had four types of clients and we delivered the newsletter in five different ways that there were 20 points of contact we had with our clients, just with our newsletters.

Brainstorming Checklist

➤ Online webpages
➤ Blogs
➤ Printed and mailed to client
➤ Inside packages if you ship goods to your clients
➤ Waiting rooms or areas at restaurants where your ideal customers are

Multiple Media Newsletters

Newsletters are supposed to be read, of course, but the more of the five senses we can engage our clients with, the better chances our message will be consumed. Plus, you will already have paid to mail the newsletter, so consider including an audio CD with the newsletter to higher-level clients. The clients that spent the most money with me received a CD in their newsletter with a personal message from me so it helped build a tighter bond between us. In some of the audio CD's, I interviewed my clients and they served as audio testimonies. Or, on occasion I would find an industry expert and interview them or even other times I would interview my own employees and we would discuss technical aspects of our repair process. (See Figure 4.6)

Figure 4.6

Here is how to lay-out a typical 4 page self mailer type of newsletter. (See Figure 4.7)

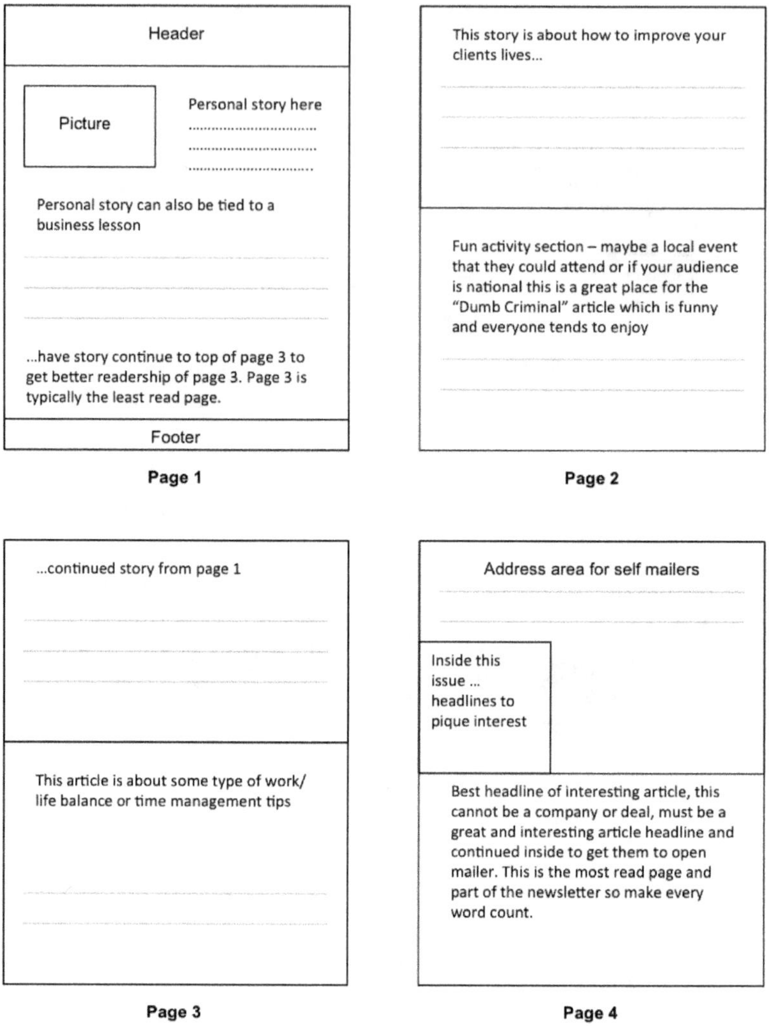

Page 1	Page 2
Header	This story is about how to improve your clients lives…
Picture — Personal story here	
Personal story can also be tied to a business lesson	Fun activity section – maybe a local event that they could attend or if your audience is national this is a great place for the "Dumb Criminal" article which is funny and everyone tends to enjoy
…have story continue to top of page 3 to get better readership of page 3. Page 3 is typically the least read page.	
Footer	
Page 1	**Page 2**

Page 3	Page 4
…continued story from page 1	Address area for self mailers
	Inside this issue … headlines to pique interest
This article is about some type of work/ life balance or time management tips	Best headline of interesting article, this cannot be a company or deal, must be a great and interesting article headline and continued inside to get them to open mailer. This is the most read page and part of the newsletter so make every word count.
Page 3	**Page 4**

Figure 4.7

Doing it yourself

You certainly can do it all yourself and here are some of the tools and methods to accomplish this.

Software - Powerpoint or publisher work great or use any software that will allow you to move pictures around easily. Don't start from scratch, use a newsletter that you like and swipe and deploy the format, then make up your own content. Make it personal and at most only 40% about work related topics.

Header – This is the first thing people are going to see, so spend some time or pay a graphic designer to make a nice one for you. It should cost you $5 on fiverr.com and someone can make you a really sharp looking one. Name it something other than your company name, this newsletter is personal and not all about your service or product.

Theme – If you use a monthly theme for your newsletter this will make putting it together quite a bit easier and require less brainpower each month. It's also a fast way to come up with topics of discussion and a way to join the conversation already going on in the mind of your client.

Sections – Plan to have 2 to 3 sections per page. You don't have to use them all each month but if you plan what you are going to put on each page it makes putting the newsletter together faster and more organized and more consistent to your clients.

Jokes – Humor is the fastest way to overcome barriers, so put humor in wherever appropriate.

Pictures – Use pictures as well as text in your content because different clients consume information in different ways. Some of them like to do a lot of reading and some will like lots of pictures, so design your content with both. A cheap place to find them is in your software clip art or online, but be aware of copyright protection.

Color – Stick with the monthly theme and remember that color increases readership and response.

Lumpy Mail – If you put something into the envelope that makes it "feel" different than a letter it will get opened up and consumed more often. Think about what I did each month with the CD I put into the envelope. Lumpy Mail usually isn't cost effective for residential HVAC or plumbing customers whose equipment isn't ripe for replacement. However, if I own or rent commercial property in a typical "strip mall" with a dozen heating/cooling units on the roof it may be well worth it.

Double readership path – Put a table of contents on the front page to give readers another way to get your information, again this increases consumption of your content.

Surveys – The most efficient way to find out what your clients needs are, is to ask them, and a survey is a great way to do this.

Wordfind – This is a creative way to have your clients engage in your content. With a little creativity and a little reward you can have your clients responding frequently.

Monthly deals – Handwritten in crayon is an outrageous way to bring attention to your monthly deals

Mailing format – Inside an envelope, with a return address to you personally at your company address, in a handwritten font, with a stamp placed a little crooked works best.

How would you like to be able to make sure your clients are actively engaged in your newsletter and have proof of it with a 24% response from your monthly list and have your newsletter actually go viral?

Swipe and Deploy – Ninja Newsletter Technique

I wanted a way to make our newsletter readers actively engage with us when they read the newsletter instead of just passively reading it and then throwing it away. I wanted a way to make it more fun and have my clients desire the newsletters every month. So I put a "Word Find" activity into our newsletter, but instead of using someone else's "Word Find" I made my own. (See Figures 4.8 and 4.9) I used MS Excel and simply put the words into it myself, but my secret ninja technique was to use words associated with my services. So this taught my clients about the terminology of the industry as well as giving them a good feeling about my services. I have a 24% rate of engagement with this activity and each month I changed it to reflect what was going on with the company. I also gave my clients a reward for responding to it. I typically used gift cards that I got from reward points from my vendors and creditors so there was only a minimal cost to me to do this for my clients.

There were some major advantages to getting my clients to fill in all of this information. One of them is that I was able to get an updated list of correct contact information and it also let me know that they were still actively involved with me. Another is that I was able to get an email address where I may have not had one. And lastly, and this one is huge – The newsletter grew my list. You see when my clients filled in the word find and then walked over to the fax machine, their co-workers wanted to find out what the excitement was all about and so they start to talk about getting a $10.00 gift card from one of their vendors. So as soon as the first fax was sent to back to me, the other employee would grab the word find, scratch out the other persons name and fill it in for himself and then sends me another fax. So now I had a newsletter that became viral and I got to grow my client contact list.

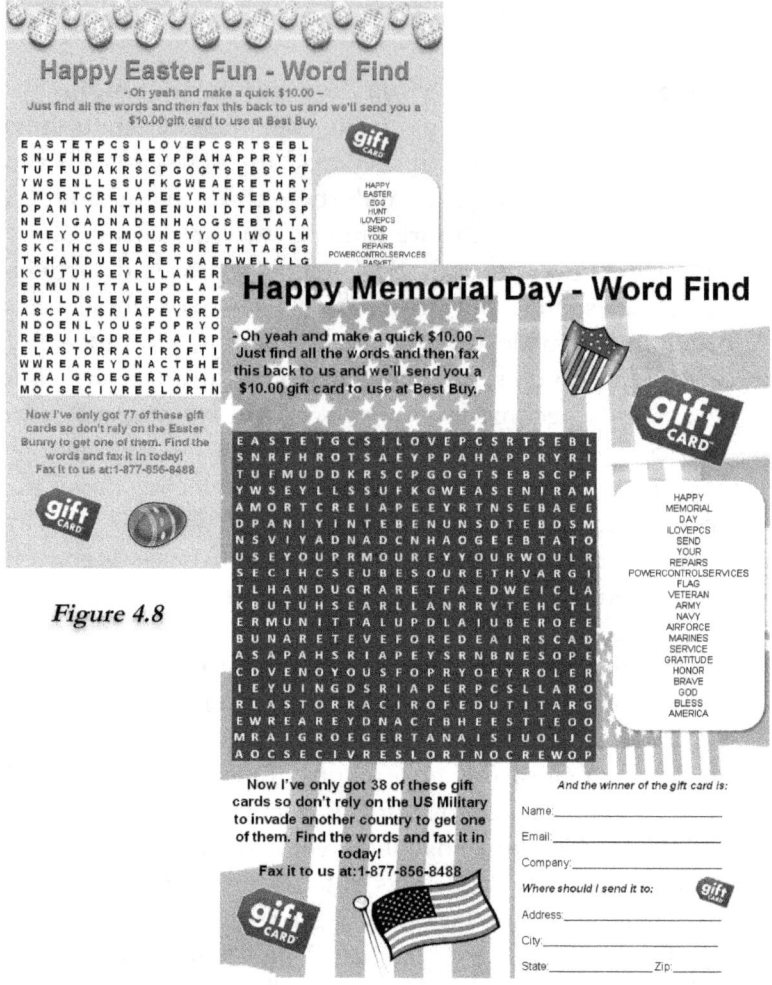

Figure 4.8

Figure 4.9

Brainstorming Checklist

What sections are you going to have in the newsletter?
What is your theme going to be for the current month?
Do you have a good place to find some jokes and humor?
Do you have any testimonials you can use?
What monthly deal are you going to put into it?
What questions would you like to have your clients answer in a survey?
Is there anything lumpy that you can put into your envelope with the newsletter?

Are you ready to take the next logical step? Schedule your contractor market assessment. So you can identify the prospects that are 600 X more likely to turn into a new customer...and it's FREE too!
Simply go to www. MEERScore.com/freeoffer and fill out the application for a 45 minute phone call with Mike Layton.

As a special bonus, this includes an additional FREE strategy session to get your customized plan for exponential growth with Walter Bergeron.

Referral Program

Your referral program will gain you new business from your second best client type, referrals from existing clients. You will have a program that takes advantage of the strong relationship you have with your existing clients.

Make it easy for them to refer - Give your clients the tools they need to do a great job to refer business to you. Give them business cards to hand out that have an irresistible offer and a call to action with a deadline. Don't simply tell them that you love referrals. Give them a message to communicate and reward them for referring, each time and every time.

Timing is important – Ask for referrals when you make a sale as well as when your client feels great about your product or service, certainly not when they have a complaint.

Drop off a business card and get a gift card – One card for another. Sure it'll cost you $5.00 or $10.00 but this will instill in your clients to always be looking for referrals and people to talk to about your company. Don't go cheap on this, it's not about affordability, it's about profitability. Don't do the "Enter for a chance to win" crap! Just give it to them right then and there. Immediate rewards for being a raving fan. This raises the bar and when (not if) but when things go wrong (and they will and always do) your clients will be so much more forgiving because you give a damn enough to give them a gift really often.

Use other premiums like a book or a coozie or a hat or a pen or anything to reward your clients for referring others to you. This is also a great way to get email addresses. You can also do these things right away in person right when your techs or plumbers are running appointments. You can sign them up and have then double opt in for the email campaign while they are at your location, it's becoming more and more about immediate gratification. If it's what they want, give it to them.

Brainstorming Checklist

Straight cash / Gift card
> ➤ Can form alliance with restaurants, other vendors to purchase gift cards at a discount
> ➤ Make it worth their while

How you can make them feel extra special?
> ➤ Special marketing to top referrers and call attention to doing this for you, this also trains your clients that they should be giving referrals and how to do business with you.

Announce it
> ➤ Newsletter
> ➤ Website
> ➤ Letter with audio cd

Example

I have a client that is in a highly commoditized industry, HVAC. His company repairs and services residential air-conditioning equipment and his referral system was in shambles. He did the typical contractor method of a refrigerator magnet that said, WE LOVE REFERRALS. And that was it. At least he was mentioning the fact that referrals were important. The problem is that asking for a referral passively and actually getting referrals are two totally different monsters. So we came up with a fantastically effective referral system for him. Step 1 was to find out when his clients were the happiest with him and it turns out it was when the client felt the cold air come back on. His clients seemed relieved that they weren't going to have to spend another night sweating it out in bed, praying for the AC to kick on and cool off the house. So his technicians made it a point to be there with the client right when the air conditioner was turned on and even went as far as standing near one of the air vents to experience that burst of cold air with his clients. It was at that exact moment that Wade's employees would very politely ask for the names of 5 neighbors that his client would give him right then and there and to send a pre prepared letter to their neighbors. So his tech carried lots of pre packaged envelopes with a marketing package already inside and the client simply wrote a few kind words on a letter and then the envelope was sealed and mailed that very day from the client's mailbox. That's a referral system. The client's neighbors almost all came to ask about the letter and his referral rates skyrocketed because of this simple little change in the system for getting referrals.

Lost Client Reactivation

Lost clients are often an overlooked category of clients, though actually the third best type of client to reintroduce to your products or services, especially if they didn't replace their system on your last visit. They already know your services so we will reintroduce them to you and let them know they have not been forgotten as well as address any past issues.

They haven't done business with you in a specified amount of time. Maybe for you that's 1 day or 1 month or 1 year, but at some point you will lose your existing clients. For most residential contractors who don't have an active Lost Client activation system (via direct mail, e-mail or outbound telemarketing) 50% of the new customers you visit every year don't do business with you again over the next 5 years. So as soon as you noticed that they are no longer doing business with you, you should begin asking them to

> A very common misconception entrepreneurs have is that clients leave because they are dissatisfied. The truth is that they feel ignored and that a company feels indifferent about them.

come back.

There is a common misconception that entrepreneurs have about the reason that their clients leave. Many entrepreneurs think that clients leave only because they are dissatisfied in some way with the service they received. Well, I must tell you that this is simply not true. Most of the time, and I encourage you to do your own research, but most of the time it has been found that the reason clients stop doing business with someone is because they feel neglected, they feel you are indifferent. They aren't even asked to do business with you and so they go somewhere else because you have never asked them to come back.

So why don't you simply ask them to come back. That's as easy as a letter to them apologizing for having done something wrong and asking for another chance. Then give them some type of incentive to come back. I think you'll find that by making this one little change you'll reap great rewards from returning clients even if you don't move forward with selling your business. Give it a try and see what happens.

I took this lost client reactivation program directly from GKIC and swiped and deployed it with minimal changes to the copy. (See Figure 4.10, 4.11,4.12 and 4.13) We implemented this program for any client that had not done work with us in six months and it is still in use today when clients hit the six-month point.

"We really want you back!"

Dear [first name],
As you can see we have included a Boomerang with this letter. Our records indicate it's been too long since we've heard from you at [company name]. **So we're giving you $388.00 in this letter just to get you back!**

Here are 3 reasons Why You Need To Return To Power Control Services and send us all of your industrial electronic equipment for repair.

Our Triple Guarantee

1. <u>Guaranteed</u> to work the first time, every time – *If your equipment doesn't arrive to you 100% fully operational we guarantee we will pay for all the costs to send it back to us as many times as necessary until we get it right.*

2. <u>Guaranteed</u> to cost less than a new replacement – *Our cost for repair will always be more affordable than replacing your broken automation equipment with new equipment.*

3. <u>Guaranteed</u> to back your equipment up with our Lifetime Warranty – *Who else backs up their repairs for a Lifetime. No one else does, they just gives you 6 months or at most 1 year. PCS has a Lifetime Warranty period, so it doesn't matter if you use your equipment right away or if you let it sit on a shelf for years before you are able to put it into service. We've got you covered.*

HURRY! Offer Expires on Halloween!(10/31/11)

Sincerely,
Walter Bergeron

P.S. Hurry and call today so we can reconnect! **We really do miss you!**

P.P.S. These $97.00 off deals expire on Halloween (10/31/11). Call me today! 1-800-962-6355

3827 Pinhook Rd. Broussard, LA 70518 | 561 Thornton Road - Suite N Lithia Springs, GA 0122
800.962.6355 (toll free) 877.856.8488 (toll free fax) | 337.232.1663 (local) 337.232.1693 (local fax)
Info@powercontrolservices.com | www.powercontrolservices.com

Figure 4.10

"Are you lost!"

Should We Send Out the Search Party?

So last week I sent you a letter with a Boomerang and now I'm sending you another one with a Compass inside. I'm concerned I haven't heard from you and I'm worried that you might be lost. **(Hence the reason for the compass.)**

As I said in the previous letter, our records indicate it's been too long since we've heard from and my guess is that we screwed things up. **So I want to make it up to you and straight up give you $197.00 off any repair. The last deal I sent to you sucked but I hope this one sucks less.**

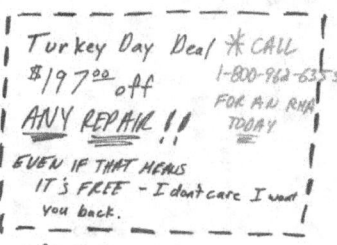

1. <u>Guaranteed</u> **to work the first time, every time** – If your equipment doesn't arrive to you 100% fully operational we guarantee we will pay for all the costs to send it back to us as many times as necessary until we get it right.

2. <u>Guaranteed</u> **to cost less than a new replacement** – Our cost for repair will always be more affordable than replacing your broken automation equipment with new equipment.

3. <u>Guaranteed</u> **to back your equipment up with our Lifetime Warranty** – Who else backs up their repairs for a Lifetime. No one else does, they just gives you 6 months or at most 1 year. PCS has a Lifetime Warranty period, so it doesn't matter if you use your equipment right away or if you let it sit on a shelf for years before you are able to put it into service. We've got you covered.

Sincerely,
Walter Bergeron

P.S. Hurry and call today so we can reconnect! **We really do miss you!**

P.P.S. This $197.00 off deal expires on Thanks giving Day. Call for an RMA today! 1-800-962-6355

3827 Pinhook Rd. Broussard, LA 70518 | 561 Thornton Road - Suite N Lithia Springs, GA 0122
800.962.6355 (toll free) 877.856.8488 (toll free fax) | 337.232.1663 (local) 337.232.1693 (local fax)
Info@powercontrolservices.com | www.powercontrolservices.com

Figure 4.11

Figure 4.12

Figure 4.13

Chapter 4/Marketing Makeover

New Client Acquisition Program

Many times businesses leap to attempting to gain new clients only to realize that new clients are the most expensive and most difficult type of client to convert. Only after using the other 3 types of client acquisition should you move to trying to gain new clients. For residential contractors, in any given 12 month period a new customer is worth 2.5 – 4 times as much as re-activated existing or inactive customer. Because revenue from new customers is always 60 – 70% of your sales, successful, economical, sustained new customer acquisition programs are the most important part of your marketing programs. While existing residential customers are more likely to respond to your marketing programs on <u>average</u> they are much less valuable than new residential customers.

Light commercial clients are a different story. They often have multiple heating/cooling systems on their buildings or their plumbing systems have to support multiple bathrooms throughout their buildings. Marketing systems aimed at uncovering one and done transactions (replacement systems for HVAC or major repairs for plumbing) that drive residential sales aren't the best solution for light commercial clients. Light commercial clients with a higher average lifetime value justify the use of programs like these.

In my own business I initiated a complete sales funnel to reach my ideal client types and help me grow the business with them. But I created a complex campaign and not just a one or two piece marketing effort. When you do this for yourself, revel in the complexity of what a campaign consists of because even if your commercial competitors can see what you are doing from the outside, they will never be able to duplicate what is going on behind the scenes. Let them try all they want and fail! It may look simple but the details are what keep this part of your marketing system successful.

I wanted my campaigns to blow my competitors away, they would send a single direct mail piece and maybe an email or possibly a salesman would make an appointment. I did an entire campaign (See Figure 4.14 and 4.15) of multiple emails, multiple direct mail pieces and then the grand finale was to ship them my secret weapon, which resulted in 100% response! I would start my campaign with multiple emails through Infusionsoft. These emails were the e-books I created.

Figure 4.14

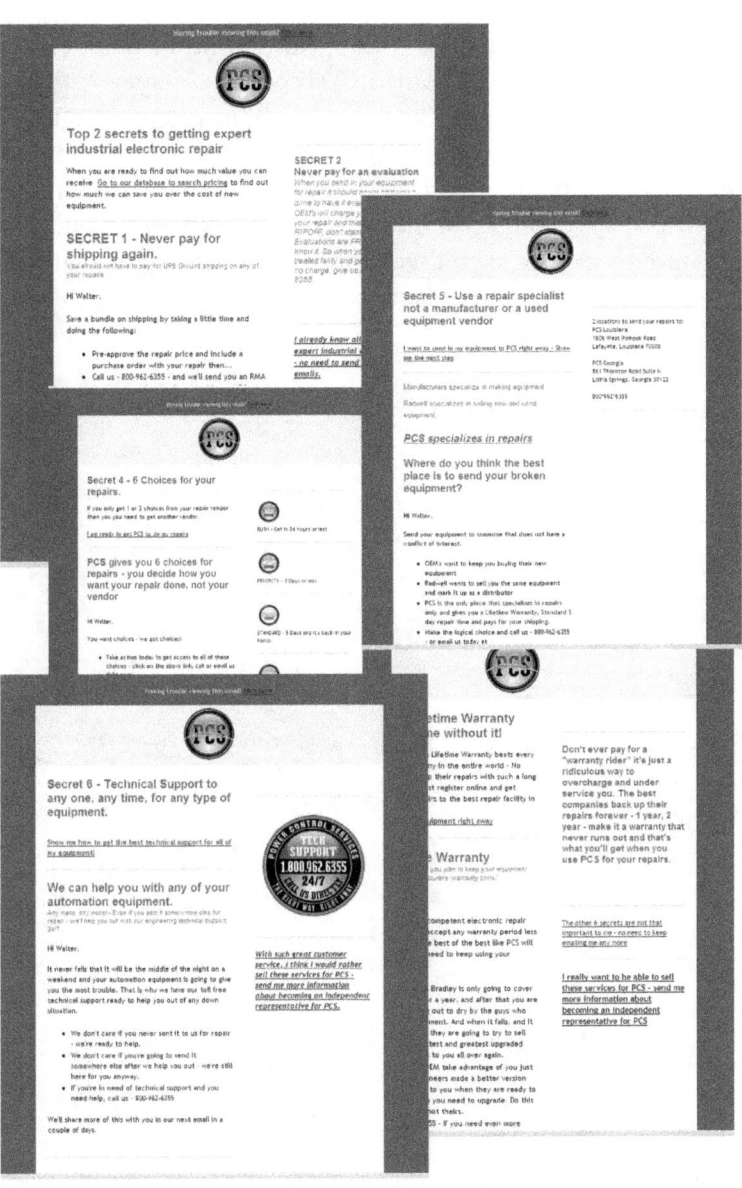

Figure 4.15

I would then follow that with a long form sales letter that had a handwritten font on yellow lined paper with copy doodles. (See Figure 4.16 and 4.17) I then added 3D pieces to get better response, but not 100% response. The email might get deleted and the direct mail pieces could be thrown away and those salesman's appointments would be cancelled at the last minute. So the secret weapon had to be deployed and this was my shock and awe package.

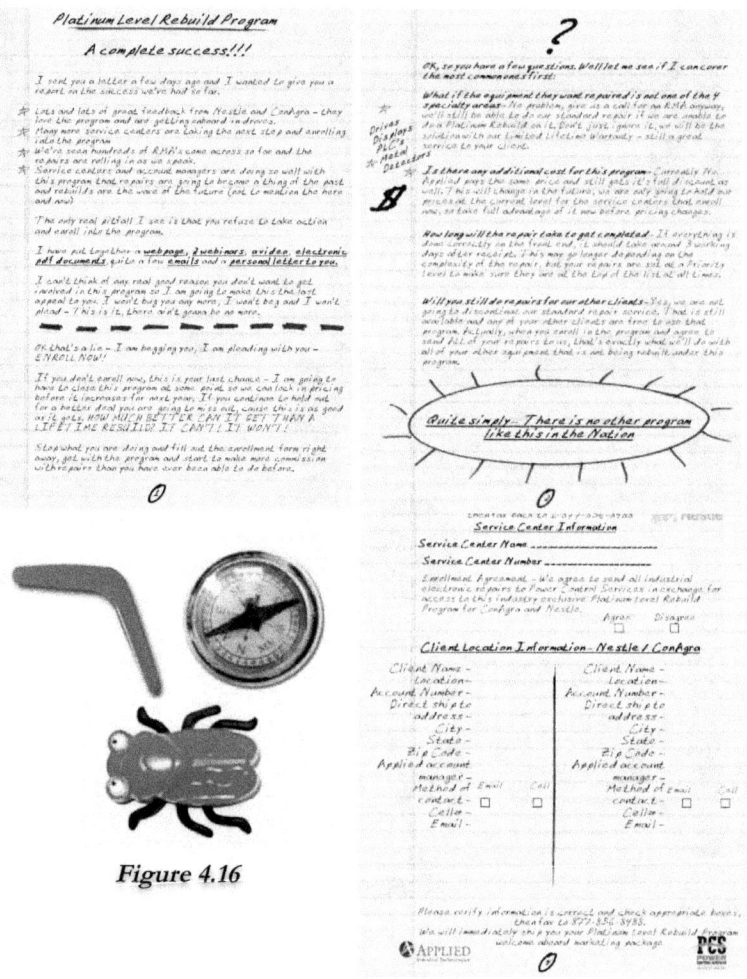

Figure 4.16

Shock and Awe Package!!
- Video
- King Cake
- Marketing message

TOP SECRET

Figure 4.17

None of my competitors would send a shock and awe package like this! I would send this package to them marked with "perishable goods, open immediately" on it. You see everyone likes to get gifts and this thing is so intriguing it is opened up 100% of the time immediately upon receipt. And when it gets opened up a video starts to play. Since I am from Louisiana, I would include a beautiful Mardi Gras king cake in it and the video gives them instructions to start enjoying the king cake while they watch a short video about my services. This thing gets results, and since I knew that these clients were worth $34,575 each I could afford to spend the $200 for each of these cases, but I also included a prepaid shipping label and I would actually get these returned to me and the client would ask for a refill on the King Cake. I had to outsmart my competitors if I was to expect to out perform their marketing and that's exactly what I did. I have a completely unfair advantage over my competitors and that's the way I like it.

Website

There are many various types of websites and each has it's own unique benefits depending on the needs of the business and the target audience it is being used for. Knowing what options are available to you and the differences between each type of website will go a long way in determining which website types will work best for your situation. For residential contractors it is critically important that your website (PPC, SEO, Mobile, etc.) be optimized to leverage your presence in your top 8-10 zip codes. Web leads that come from the parts of your market where your relative market share is less than 2% (often less than 1%) of the owner occupied dwellings actually shrink the value of your business because new clients there are on average worth considerably less than new customers in your primary zip codes. Remember, every zip code is a primary zip code for somebody. When your website competes for new customers in areas where someone else has a relative market share that is 600 x higher than yours what you are usually getting is some else's overflow, not good prospects for you.

Single page Websites

This type of website is just as it describes, it's a single page for a quick splash for your one specific product or service. (See Figure 4.18) It won't have great visibility on search engines but what this type of site is great at is to link to ebooks, other websites, downloads and to direct your client in a laser focused manner to what you want them to do, what action you want them to take next.

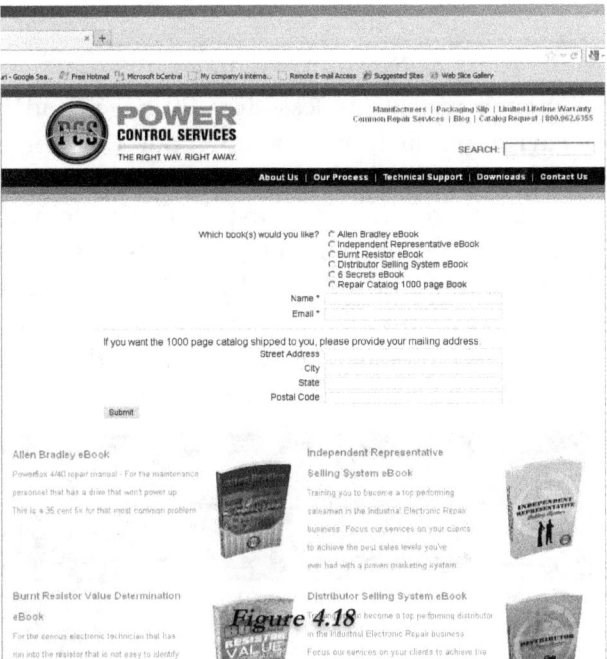

Figure 4.18

Example:

I took our standard catalog unresponsive website and put in a single page website to promote a lead capture web-form for each type of client and linked them to Infusionsoft with 5 Free E-Books that we call our "Client Value Building Library"

Simple Websites

A simple website is less than 20 pages and has the standard navigation such as Home, About Us, Contact Us, Blog and the remaining pages contain information about your business. (See Figure 4.19) This type of website allows for much easier search engine rankings and is easy to update yourself. It is meant to be a credibility building marketing tool as well as general information about you and your company. The more often you update this type of site with relevant and valuable content, the better search engines will rank it.

Figure 4.19

Complex Website

This type of website takes the simple website and ramps it up to include customized branding elements and videos. (See Figure 4.20) It will typically get better search engine rankings because at this level it is usually maintained and updated by an outside 3rd party vendor specializing in website design, creation and rankings. You will be able to make changes to assist with rankings but the heavy lifting is better left to the pros that designed it for you.

This type of site can more easily support advanced elements and pages such as videos, audios, membership portals, opt-in pages, retargeting, etc... Lots and lots of options to be looked at, just be aware that at this level the behind the scenes work level is much more intensive so that your clients have a greater and more rewarding experience when visiting this type of website.

Figure 4.20

Squeeze Pages

This type of website is a very focused website with only one purpose, to engage with your prospect about a single topic (like IAQ, Water Filtration, Solar, Generators) or action. (See Figure 4.21) Also referred to as a landing page, it is designed to attract a prospect and get them to give you their contact information in exchange for some type of value.

The value you give them can be in any form really, but the most popular gifts are information such as videos, audios, webinars, teleseminars, pdf downloads, ebooks or possibly a strategy session phone call. Depending on how your back end sales funnel works this type of page will be your entry point to an entire campaign.

Figure 4.21

Specialty Websites

Mobile websites are a specially formatted website that is designed specifically to be viewed by mobile devices you're your smartphone or tablet or anything in between. Your clients are moving toward viewing information in this manner and its best to do all you can to allow your websites to be viewed in as many formats as possible so when designing or updating your website make sure it is able to be viewed by mobile devices.

Membership or Service Agreement websites are another type of specialty site that allow you to engage with your clients in a more personal and specific manner. This type of website is a great way to deliver training materials, information products or any type of customized engagement with your clients. Later on we will discuss continuity programs and membership websites are a great tool to be able to deliver these types of programs with.

Moving Ahead

What you are going to find is that the more complex your marketing system gets, the more complex your online needs will be. There may have been a time when one type of website would be sufficient, but that time has long gone. Now you need to have a combination of website types to engage and to stay engaged with your prospects and clients. You will need multiple websites, multiple types of websites and an efficient back end software and team to help you develop and maintain it if you are driven to have the most efficient and productive marketing system you can have that integrates an online presence.

No matter what type or combination of types of websites you use you will need to stay educated in their use and best practices as well as what type to use and when to use it. My recommendation is that this is where you typically have two choices. Either get really good at it yourself, just keep in mind that this may not be the best and most profitable use of your time. Choice number two is to find a qualified professional website service, of which there are millions of available worldwide, and have them design and maintain your web presence.

> Are you ready to take the next logical step? Schedule your contractor market assessment. So you can identify the prospects that are 600 X more likely to turn into a new customer…and it's FREE too!
> Simply go to www. MEERScore.com/freeoffer and fill out the application for a 45 minute phone call with Mike Layton.
>
> As a special bonus, this includes an additional FREE strategy session to get your customized plan for exponential growth with Walter Bergeron.

Customer Service

How your company handles clients is critical to client retention. Now there are many ways that customer service ties into marketing. Such as in person greetings and transactions, phone transactions and email transactions. All of these types of transactions must be planned and scripted. There should be no accidents on how your clients are handled and spoken to and how your employees represent your company to your clients. You should start by scripting out all interactions between you and your clients and how you want each of these situations handled. Very few successful residential HVAC or Plumbing contractors don't use scripted greetings and scripts for booking appointments. Your customer service agents will be more successful if you use unique tracking numbers for your most common campaigns and calls to those tracking numbers lead your agents to use the appropriate script for a replacement system inquiry vs a tune-up or water heater flush call.

When a client calls with an order or a question or a complaint or for any reason, you should have your employees trained on how to handle each and every communication. If done properly these interactions should eventually, if not immediately, result in another sale or referral or testimonial.

In my own business an important area to us was our incoming calls, so we got together with the phone sales doctor and developed scripts that we make our customer service representatives follow. We had mystery shoppers that call them and we recorded the calls and listened to them monthly. To help train the CSR's I made them a CD to listen to on their way to and from work, we called it Automobile University and instead of paying them I gave them incentives to complete listening to the CD. As an example I would record a message somewhere in the one hour CD with either a code word or an outright gift to tell them to be the first one to come my office and tell me the code word and I would give them a $50.00 gift card. That is a really inexpensive way to motivate employees to training them and have them compete with each other to actually do the training. I also had the monthly CD's transcribed and we made a booklet out of them to help train new employees about how to handle different types of calls.

With today's technology, every call can be recorded and analyzed quickly and cheaply. You should be able to identify every call that was an appointment opportunity but did NOT result in an appointment. You've spent $50, $100 even $250 to make that call happen. On average, a new customer is worth $800 to $2500 to the typical plumber or HVAC contractor (maybe a lot more if it's a new commercial customer). Someone in your organization needs be given the responsibility to call and try to save every opportunity that was NOT booked before close of business. The person making the callback should not be the person who failed to book the call the first time. If you are large enough to have a call center or customer service manager, make them responsible for saving the call. If you aren't that big, you should make the call. Those Missed Opportunity notifications can go straight to your smart phone if you are out running calls.

Example: (See Figure 4.22) This is my business card back, with offer and deadline and not the same old stuff everyone else is doing. The front is standard and needs some sprucing up to make more outrageous.

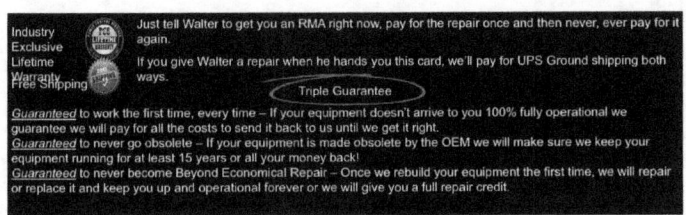

Figure 4.22

Sample Incoming Call Script

1. Greeting. Thank you for calling Power Control Services this is_____speaking how can I help you?"

2. I can help you. May I ask your name?_____

3. Wow Welcome. _____, let me be the first to welcome you to Power Control Services.

4. **What prompted you to call today?** _____

You made the **right decision** calling today.

5. Repeat the problem in their words with urgency.

6. Provide the <u>SOLUTION.</u> Let me get some information from you so I can send you a quote to include your total investment I will send that to you right now while I'm on the phone with you. Did you get it? Great open it up let's review_____. Or, I'm going to send this to you in the next_____. What's your email or fax? Are you at this email address/fax right now? Or, I'm going to call you back to review this so I can get this order in right away and if I can do it by _____ here's what you can expect_____.

Try to do everything on the spot or same day or next earliest date/time. The tone is important speed now urgency.

Who is the decision maker?_____

7. **Who can we thank for referring you?** _____

Include referral reward if you have one.

8. Close Properly The Contract. Thank you once again _____, you made the **right decision** in calling us today, we look forward to speaking to you_____ at _____. If for any reason you need to reschedule would you please **promise** to call_____so that we can give that time to someone else that's waiting?

[Wait for their reply]

This time has been <u>**reserved**</u> just for you.

9. Wow Closing The Final Hug:
1) Did I answer all your questions?
2) Is there anything else I can help you with?
3) Thank you for calling.

Signs

Perception is reality and if you have signs of any type then this program will remove the platitudes on your signs and replace them with direct marketing based signage.

Here are some of the biggest lessons learned in developing signs that produce a substantial ROI. (See Figure 4.23)

1. Yard Signs – get them done by a professional.

2. The bigger the better – Size matters!

3. Keep the typeface consistent and all caps are difficult to read at a glance

4. Remember that the focal point of the sign is just above the center top to bottom and centerline from left to right.

5. Don't use too much reverse type

6. Be as specific on the signs as you can, don't use general terms

7. Explain the things that are not obvious

8. Don't waste time explaining the obvious

9. Make the sign copy positive, not negative sounding

10. Add benefits

11. Color sells better than black and white

12. Plan the sign location for highest visibility

13. Make the signs consistent with each other

Figure 4.23

No budget

I have to tell you that this is exactly where I started out when I started my own direct marketing results triangle and direct marketing system. One of the immediate and power tactics you can use if you have no budget is to raise your prices. I know this is typically a barrier to people because they think that they can't increase their prices. But I would urge you to try smaller price increases first. I tried a 15% increase in my prices and no one even noticed. My clients weren't specifically paying attention to exactly how much I was charging them, so when I raised my prices 15% I got an immediate cash infusion. When that happened, I was able to spend more money to use on my marketing system.

Advanced Marketing Systems

This is going to set your even farther apart from what your competitors are doing and gain you what I like to call an unfair advantage in your industry. This is such a great way to tip the odds in your favor and give you home field advantage. Who wants to play or do business where everything is fair and equal, I don't, I want to give myself every unfair advantage I can to make my businesses successful.

These advanced marketing systems will also make your business more valuable to potential buyers. We touched on this in the foundational section. When buyers are looking at your business they are going to require that your business has documented and proven marketing systems in place with great ROI to back it up, especially when these are 8 figure plus transactions. You can make your business valuation multiples higher because you have made your marketing system into one of your greatest and most valuable assets. Now maybe at smaller levels you can get away with having marketing happen by accident, but that is not the case when you want to be able to get top dollar at $10 million plus. When I was selling my last company there was a time during the due diligence process where we sat at a large conference room table. My attorneys, their attorneys, my CPA, their CPA as well as other business advisors where it was time to show them what our systems look like. So we went into the company library and started hauling out huge armfuls of three ring binders, and each one of these binders contained one piece of our marketing system. So when everything was laid out on the table we had dozens and dozens of binders stacked up on top of each other to show them and to demonstrate that we had a proven marketing system. This demonstration blew them away and was one of the reasons that I was able to get a 7X multiplier on earnings for the company. So having a great marketing system in place not only adds value to the sales of the business, it also makes things operate a whole lot more smoothly and really sets you apart from your competitors as well as makes a huge impact to your buyers.

Not only will you be able to command a higher price for your company but you'll set your business apart when buyers are comparing buying your company versus someone else's company. In a sea of sameness you will put your business in a category of one by having these advanced marketing pieces in place and providing your business with proven ROI.

You will be able to buy businesses at top dollar and still make that price a bargain. The way this works is by finding businesses to buy that have underperforming marketing systems. Among residential contractors this usually means a marketing system that emphasizes branding across a wide area 80+ zip codes instead of domination in 10 good zip codes. If branding works, its' turning into more new customers. Where your branding really works is in just a few zip codes. Give this some thought, how often do you encounter other businesses that have a poor or even non-existent marketing system? Pretty much every time you walk into a business, right? So even if you have to pay top dollar, which we will certainly try to avoid, but even if you do, when you go into a business with a poor marketing system and deploy your proven, advanced marketing system your new acquisition becomes immediately more valuable and then soon becomes even more profitable when you put in place your marketing system.

Lastly, even if you decide not to sell your company, you will still be able to grow it profitably through organic growth with marketing, exponential growth through acquisitions and then to combine these two methods to build yourself an empire.

Make sure you have done all of the foundational marketing from the previous section before you start working on the advanced marketing section. Because they will build on each other and many of the advanced marketing systems will require that you have done all the work in the foundational marketing section. Otherwise it will get very overwhelming for you and you won't get started or worse yet your foundational pieces won't be there and instead of getting a system up and running all you will have is poorly developed pieces of an ineffective mess. Do the work. Get the foundation set up first.

Direct Marketing Client Lifecycle

Now in the Foundational Marketing section we briefly covered the diagram called the Direct marketing Client Lifecycle, but I wanted to make sure that we went over this in the advanced section so take a look at the diagram. This applies more for commercial clients than residential customers. If you are primarily a residential contractor and you've built marketing systems that are successfully building your residential business, then maybe the reason your commercial side isn't growing very much is because you haven't looked at your commercial clients like this. (See Figure 4.24) On the left hand side you will notice that this is where our interaction with our 4 types of clients begins. Remember they are our existing clients, which are our best and easiest to sell to. There are our referral clients, second best, our lost clients and our new clients. This is in order of importance. All of these clients feed into our sales conversion process and a certain percentage of them will convert into buyers at any one given time. Then we deliver and satisfy, upsell and then we repeat the process. Two things we didn't cover previously were the top right hand section of the diagram where you see that we are going to innovate and watch for trends. These areas are where we make sure we don't stagnate in our marketing and sales. This is how we avoid becoming Blockbuster or Circuit City and miss major market trends that change the market and make sure we change with it instead of getting left behind.

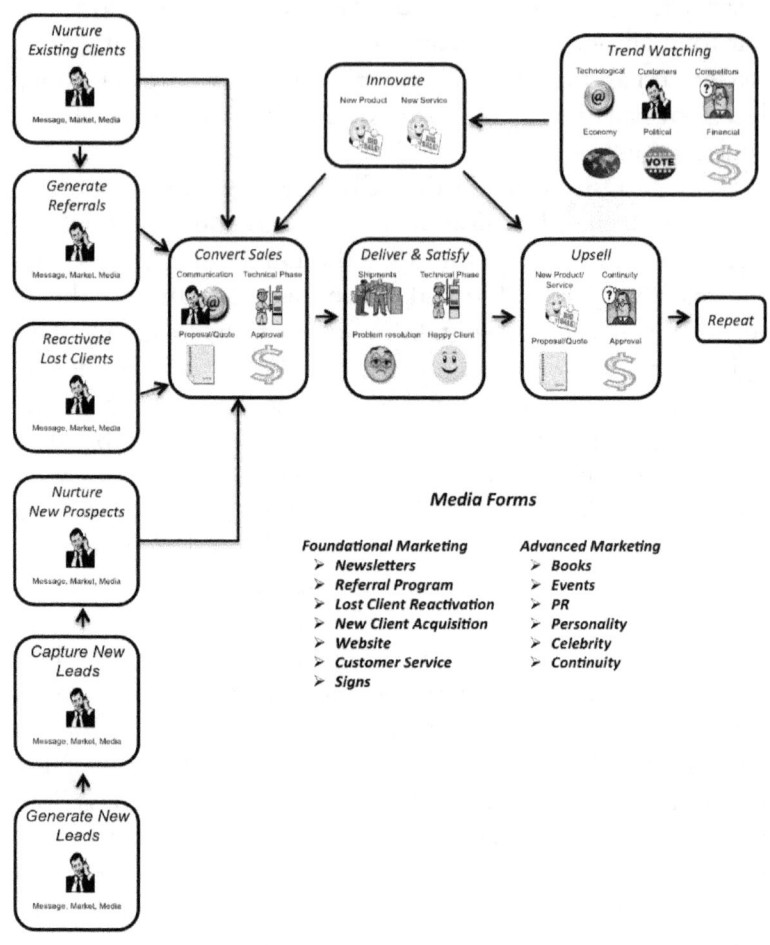

Media Forms

Foundational Marketing
- Newsletters
- Referral Program
- Lost Client Reactivation
- New Client Acquisition
- Website
- Customer Service
- Signs

Advanced Marketing
- Books
- Events
- PR
- Personality
- Celebrity
- Continuity

Figure 4.24

Books

The most effective way to build a better trust-based relationship with your clients is through publishing books. Please keep in mind that these are books to be used to position you as an expert in your field and not the great American novel you always wished you could write. The purpose of these books is to drive clients to you and pre-position you as the authority in your industry or profession. Notice I used the word these and not this. That's because you must write multiple books and today that is easier than ever with so many tools at your disposal.

First, these books will be self-published, meaning that there is no need to go out and find a publisher. (See Figure 4.25) To make this easy, Amazon has a company called Createspace and this is all that they do. You simply upload or create a book cover, upload your pdf book content and then tell them how many you want printed. There are a few caveats I didn't mention but in essence that is all there is to it. The cost is less than $3.00 for a 150 page book and you can order a few or many thousands and Createspace can fulfill your needs. Then these books can be given as thank you gifts to existing clients. These books can serve as the tool you give to your existing clients to help them refer even more clients to you. They can serve as a gift to give to lost clients to reactivate them. They can become a lead generation magnet for new clients. These books can become the backbone of your marketing system because they can deliver your message to your clients with tremendous levels of credibility and help build a high level of trust that your competitors are too lazy to copy. In my own business I did multiple books and I used a number of different formats. Sometimes I would create books to bring on my own new employees, we would hire independent representatives through our distribution sales model to come in and sell our services. So I wrote a book on how it would be advantageous for new independent representatives to come on board with us versus going to work for my competitor or going to work for someone else in a similar industry. I would write detailed books on specific products such as Allen Bradley, which is a specific manufacturer in our industry. I would write books to make our company the expert on those specific types of equipment. I would also do generic books on electronic repair such as burned resistors. I would also go on to write a bestseller that described my journey to the marketer of the year and then eventually to sell my business for eight figures. So we would write multiple books to make ourselves an expert in our field.

Here are some ways you can write your business quickly and easily to position yourself as the expert in your industry.

Figure 4.25

Ways to write your book quickly

The Interview

This method works well if you don't like to write. Simply jot down the top ten questions you want to answer for your client. Some examples of great questions would be the same ones you answered when you created your USP.

Why should your client use you versus any other option available to them?
You already answered this in your USP creation, you're simply going to go into much greater detail.

Why is your product or service so much better?

What things are they thinking about your product or service that they are not saying to your face?
You already know that there are conversations going on when you are not present, they are speaking about your products and services. And you probably have a good idea what those conversations are like so you want to bring those things up proactively and answer them on your own terms instead of them doing these things behind closed doors. This is a fantastic way to overcome objections.

What does it feel and look like when your product or service is used at it's best?
When things go absolutely right you want to describe that in detail including the feelings your clients will have when using your product or service.

What does it feel and look like when your product or service is used at it's worst?
Conversely, you also want to say and describe what it feels like when things are at their worst. This is when you handle objections up front, when you handle these problems on the front end. You will be able to let your clients know just how well you can do things and make sure that they understand that there will be problems. Admit the problems. Then let them know how you solve those problems in the book is a fantastic place to put those things.

Then, simply record yourself answering these questions and get it transcribed on fiverr.com and "BAM"

---

you have the makings of your book. Now take it and edit out the really terrible stuff you know isn't good and put it into chapters. Now print out this book, yes print it out, and give it to your 10 closest family, friends and clients, especially those that will be happy to give you constructive criticism about your book. These copies are then compiled and used as a second edit of your book. You can then either do more self-editing or pay an editor to do it for you. I believe Createspace also has packages where you can use their professional editors to do that for you and the price is very reasonable. But, if you have zero budget, then edit it yourself and then get it published on createspace.com

How-To Book

This is simply more detailed and tailored for a less skilled audience of the processes and procedures you use in your business to do things for your clients. In essence, it is a lite version of your trade process. Now you don't want to give away too much, but what you are doing is showing your clients all you go through to do the work or produce the product you produce. Many times when they see just how much work goes into doing what it is you do, they get overwhelmed and instead of trying to do it themselves which is what is the barrier to doing this type of book many times, instead the client understands that they don't want to or simply are not capable of doing this amount or level of skill of work and they send their business to you.

Daily Journal

This is how I wrote my fourth book. Each day when I came to work I would write down what was going on with my current project, at that time I was in the middle of a large marketing effort, so I wrote about everything I was doing with my marketing system. For you this might be how you manufacture a part, or how you prepared for a case or whatever it is that you do, but you write down your major accomplishments each and every day. You also write down what you were thinking about and especially you want to write down any struggles you are having and how you overcome those struggles. At the end of 90 days you should have enough content for a book. Then edit, send out for editing and then publish as listed above.

Co-Authoring

This is how I wrote this book, my fifth. After working with an HVAC client I decided that HVAC and plumbing contractors were a vertical market with thousands of business owners who could benefit from my experience. I sought out a partner (Mike Layton from Stochastic Marketing) with industry experience and unique services that complemented my own and we wrote this book together to serve residential HVAC and plumbing contractors specifically.

Here is another method, use an existing template and fill in the blanks with a few sentences in each area. Here is the template:

Book Template – Non-Fiction – Expert Author
Introduction
- **Define the problem** – The reason this book, challenges, well defined "why" of this book
- **The world is changing** – global trends in your topic, how is the world changing for your topic
- **The new model, reality, opportunity** – here is your quick overview of your solution
- **Your quick story** – Just a couple of sentences of two parts to your story – the struggle and then the success
- **It's possible, You can too** – the big promise of what they are going to be able to do
- **The reason to keep reading** – The big "WHY" to keep reading, how this book is going to change their paradigm about the problem, be inspirational, give an inspirational message of why to keep reading

- **Quick call to action** – Tell them what you are going to tell them in this book, a quick overview and then a sneak peak at one of the details you will share with them.
- **How to read this book** – This type of book needs to let the reader know it's OK to use as a textbook and mark it up and highlight the best parts and fold over the edges. It's meant to be used and abused.

Chapter 1
- **Current state of topic** – Similar to defining the problem and how the world is changing, just with lots more detail.
- **How things have changed** – Similar to world is changing just with much more detail and excitement
- **The bad news** – details of the bad part of the change.
- **New Approach** – reveal the way you approach the topic as the new approach.
- **Who wins and who loses** – Talk about what the winners do – your solution and then what the losers do – not your solution or doing nothing
- **How I figured it all out** – More of your struggle story – more revealing than intro – solution search part of your story – a couple of paragraphs.

Chapter 2
- **My story of struggle** – beginning days of struggle, couple of pages of struggle story.
- **Story of finding solution** – this is a teaching part of the story, your solution search and set you up as the expert
- **My success and student's successes** – Expand your story of success of yourself and then maybe your students if you have that story.

Chapter 3
- **Here's the solution Framework** - introduce the solution framework

- **Framework summary** – 1 paragraph at most on each part of the solution – big picture overview
- **The big obstacles** – Address all obstacles to your solution

Chapter 4
- **Framework** – have 1 chapter on each part of your framework

Chapter 5
- **Framework** – have 1 chapter on each part of your framework

Chapter 6
- **Framework** – have 1 chapter on each part of your framework

Chapter 7
- **Framework** – have 1 chapter on each part of your framework

Chapters 8 and on-(As many as you need to cover your solution)
- **Framework** – have 1 chapter on each part of your framework

Conclusion
- **Recap** – A couple of pages to cover again what was just said – Tell them what you told them.
- **1st Thing** – Now what you do as soon as you finish this book
- **Meaningful story** – Examples of you doing it or someone else doing it, a touching heartfelt story
- **Motivational close** – rock this close with motivation for them to take action, lift them up and inspire them and make them move on it right away.

Events & Home Shows

Getting your clients into a place where you can sell to them in a one-to-many environment is so effective that entire industries exist just to do this. You will have a new way to introduce new and existing products and services to all of your client types (existing, referral, lost and new) and achieve higher sales in a condensed time period. Events (for commercial clients) can take the shape of small 2 or 3 person group tours of your facility or office to great events with thousands of people in an exhibit hall, all there to see you. Likewise, Home Shows can bring thousands of homeowners into a show where they can "kick the tires" in a relaxed environment. No matter what the event looks like it can be a tremendously valuable way for you to build stronger client relationships and boost your business sales.

Customer Appreciation Event

This type of event is done at least annually. (See Figure 4.26) You invite as many of your past and current clients to your location to tour it and get to know your employees as well as get them more familiar with your business. You also request your vendors to participate and have them pay for the expenses and provide prizes for you to give to your clients. The other part of this is that anyone that brings a guest from another company (or their neighbor if its are residential customer gets a prize, this is a part of the referral process. Here are some of the details. Hold the event during the spring or fall, not during the frigid winter or sweltering heat of the summer. A Friday works best; people tend to be more at ease. Hold over the lunch hour and serve food, 11 – 2 works for most people's lunch period. Everyone gets door prizes for attending which are usually premiums from you and all of your vendors.

During your client invitation process you schedule a 20-minute private meeting with each of them (if they are a light commercial client). This is when you do your presentation of your services and schedule a time to meet with them again and get more business. This presentation is more of an in person survey to see what their needs are, straight from them. Then when you schedule your next meeting, you sell them what they need.

You politely strong-arm your vendors into participating and paying a small fee to compensate you for the expenses of a tent, chairs, tables, and all other expenses. The vendors are also required to bring one larger prize to give away and a small premium to give to each attendee. The vendors get a 10 minute presentation time as well as you personally introduce each of them to your clients. Each vendor gets a table/booth area to present their products as well as a list of invitees and attendees at the end of the event. We also gave each vendor a glowing recommendation letter and a video testimonial. This was for them to use in their own marketing. This was a bonus they didn't expect – under promise and over deliver. At the end of the event we also presented each vendor with a framed certificate of appreciation, took pictures and do a press release for them. Your vendors can be a terrific ally to you. Just expect them to do the same for you.

For your clients, of course you are going to dress nicely and greet them as they arrive, give them a door prize for attending, show them the food and drinks (no alcohol) and then let them mingle. At noon you do a quick thank you and open up lunch and invite everyone to eat. During this time you will do your private meetings and schedule your follow up meetings. Present awards to your vendors and give each of them a few minutes on the microphone to do a presentation to your clients, this is good to do when everyone is sitting and eating, this is a working lunch.

Figure 4.26

Virtual Events

There are also some highly productive events that you can put on virtually such as webinars and teleseminars. They are super cost effective plus you have the advantage of recording them and then turning them in to video DVD's, audio CD's, web replays, blogs, etc. Virtual events aren't just for commercial clients. Hopefully you are collecting the e-mail address from every residential customer so you can e-mail or text them appointment confirmations, service reminders etc. Why not invite them to Virtual Events like a webinar on the benefits Indoor Air Quality, Duct Sealing, Water Filtration, Smart Thermostats, etc.? Inviting 2,000 customers to a webinar on In Door Air Quality with a series of e-mails may only get 20 to attend. But those 20 are prime prospects for a face-to-face presentation during their next service call.

How do you create one?

The easiest way to create a virtual event is to choose an area of knowledge that solves a problem for your client. You already have a list of the problems you client has when you created your USP so choose one of those topics to speak on and give great value. Here is an outline that works well to both give tremendous value to your client as well as to lead into a further call to action or a sale.

1. The Setup
    a. Position the webinar as a tutorial
    b. Give them specific instruction to take notes
    c. Tell them what you are going to tell them
    d. Give a quick countdown 5,4,3,2,1 then start the presentation.
2. The Focus
    a. Paint a mental picture with an opening statement like "Imagine if this happened to you…"

b. Ask "What if.." questions to lead them to a logical conclusion of their problem
3. The Skeptics
   a. Address the skepticism you know they are going to have "Does this sound like a stretch?"
   b. Use a story formatted in a feel, felt, found format. I used to feel like..., then I felt... when I found...
4. The Reveal
   a. Reveal to them in a 100% truthful way the big discovery or secret that you found that got you the specific results in your feel, felt, found story.
5. Teaching
   a. Now you are going to teach them all the parts of your process or product or service.
   b. Three teaching points is a great format to use and give them some great value for their time. Don't hold back give them tremendous information.
6. The Offer
   a. Structure your offer straight-forward with no shenanigans.
   b. Here's what I have for you
   c. Here's what it will help you accomplish
   d. Here's what I want you to do next
   e. Introduce your solution
   f. Describe the benefits of using your solution
   g. Give the price
   h. Give a call to action with multiple ways to respond
   i. Give a great guarantee
   j. Give a deadline
   k. Put the "Buy It Now" button where they can easily take action.

Public Relations

Free publicity in any area of the country is very powerful. Whether your clients are local or national or both, publicity through news media, television, radio or magazines adds tremendous credibility and builds trust with your clients. There are many advantages to publicity, it can be cheap, it provides instant credibility, it's very fast to get to the market, it can be really fun and boosts you to a celebrity status within your market. P.R. is third party validation of who you are, this validates your place in the market, it gives you relevance and credibility. Marketing only, leaves you with a lack of credibility. So you really need P.R. too.

The best way to position yourself for great public exposure is to solve a problem and that's the place to start your public relations adventure. Make a list of problems that your clients have, you have lots of them already done with the creation of your USP in the foundational marketing section of this book. Then you need to tie that problem into what's currently hot in the news or what is always of interest in your market, the most common questions in your market. Then write a great headline about this problem and solution.

The headline is the starting point to getting the media to notice you. I have included a great starting point full of dozens of fill in the blank headlines you can use. Once you have a great headline then you need to write your press release. I have an example that GKIC did when I won Marketer of the Year, which got me lots of great press exposure.

Submit the press release to the many press release distribution sites available. You can do this in three different stages as you build your credibility. First, start off with the online free distribution sites, then move to the low cost sites and then finally on to the premium sites like Prweb. There are literally thousands of places to distribute press releases and all it takes is a quick search on line to find many of them. Start free and then move toward paid points of distribution.

Once you have them distributed online, offline uses a very similar template as online. One page, no cover sheet and never more than one page. Submit them to your local papers first and then build from there. Once you are published you can use the media credentials to build trust and credibility.

Taking this process another step further, you will take your press release and turn it into an article with great content to be used by more media. A great plan is to take a press release and submit it to radio and television stations and give notice that you allow interviews. These media are always looking to fill up with content so you should easily be able to get into local radio and television spots with good content. Then during the interview you give great content and let the host sell your products for you. Now you have even more media exposure, which perpetuates the cycle of trust. Add these media credentials to your products and content and you have a higher level of trust built with your audience.

Mass media credentials applied to direct marketing system yields highest trust.

POWER
CONTROL SERVICES

THE RIGHT WAY. RIGHT AWAY.

FOR IMMEDIATE RELEASE

Power Control Services' Walter Bergeron Voted as
Glazer-Kennedy Insider's Circle™ 2012 Marketer of the Year

Lafayette, LA, April 24, 2012 — Today, the Glazer-Kennedy Insider's Circle™ announced that Walter Bergeron of Power Control Services Inc. was chosen as their Marketer of the Year winner.

Mr. Bergeron was selected from over 50,000 members of the Glazer-Kennedy Insider's Circle™ as a winner of the prestigious Marketer of the Year award. The Glazer-Kennedy Insider's Circle™ is an exclusive group of like-minded entrepreneurs, business people, and managers who want to increase their reach, maximize their profits and create for themselves a better, more rewarding lifestyle.

"I was humbled to be selected as a winner of the Marketer of the Year award for the Glazer-Kennedy Insider's Circle™. Just to be nominated for the award from such a prestigious group of information marketers is truly an honor," said Walter Bergeron, Chief Executive Officer of Power Control Service Inc.

Mr. Bergeron was selected after completing a rigorous application process. He and seven other finalists presented at the annual GKIC SUPER CONFERENCE and the winner was selected at the conclusion of the event by their peers.

Mr. Bergeron was voted on and announced as a winner on Sunday April 22nd, just to be recognized and qualify as a finalist is an outstanding achievement, but to win is an honor few have managed to accomplish. "This is like a Cinderella story since I have only truly been active with this group for about 7 months, to stand here today as their selected winner is an honor I am humbled to accept" said Mr. Bergeron.

Marketing expert Dan Kennedy lead this elite group of marketers who meet each year at the world renowned Glazer-Kennedy Insider's Circle™ Super Conference. Each year the Super Conference brings together successful marketers from across the world enabling marketing entrepreneurs to gather and exchange new information, new discoveries and share "what's working now," as well as to network and make new contacts. This year's Super Conference was held from April 18-22 in Dallas, TX.

Power Control Services rebuilds industrial electronic equipment for the nations' top manufacturers. This service allows manufacturers to reduce maintenance cost and to be able compete more easily with global competition and help to keep products proudly Made in the USA.

Figure 4.27

Personality

Most businesses are quite boring to their clients, yes you are probably very boring to your clients if all you talk about is your industry and how good you are at it. The problem with being boring is that you are trying to form a tighter relationship with your client and that requires you to let your client into your personal life a little. People buy from people and the stronger your relationship with your clients, means that they will buy more and more often from you.

Now this doesn't mean you have to invite your clients to your birthday party at your house or have them over for Sunday barbeque every week, but it does mean they need to know more about you. Part of being considered as an expert is your journey to get there and your clients want to know how you got there and what struggles you went through. They want to know that you are like them and that things were not always easy for you. They want to know that you earned your stripes and got to where you are now with some struggle, how you found your solution and then only after you've gotten through the struggle can you tell them about your successes and how these struggles and success relates to them.

Here's how to develop your personality through your story:

First you'll need to write down what message you want to convey to your clients through your story, because you probably have many stories of struggle then success. You'll need to tell the story that best conveys which message you want to get across to your clients.

In my industrial repair business I wanted to tell my clients that cheap parts are causing major breakdowns to their equipment, but if that is all I did was say that to them, they would never listen. "That message would go in one ear and out the other", as my Mom would often tell me. So I told them about my work on an aircraft carrier during the Gulf War in the 90's and how things were bleak and the nuclear

---

reactor plant was down and captain was screaming down to get him power.

The next step is to start with your story of struggle. This is the "rags" part of your "Rags to Riches" story. Start with your pain and describe the problem in detail.

I started my story with being at war on an aircraft carrier in the middle of the Persian Gulf with the captain of the ship breathing down our necks and he needed power to launch aircraft.

Then your story goes into your search for a solution.

My story continues with looking into large cabinets full of electronics with a flashlight.

Then your story finishes with your successes and the lesson you want to convey.

My story ends with triumphantly finding the parts that failed, getting the nuclear reactor back up and running and telling my audience that this could all have been avoided if they used good parts, like my company does with all of the their equipment when they use our services.

What I am really saying here is that this does not just apply to when you are trying to sell your goods and services. It applies when you are talking about partnerships, it applies when you are talking about building relationships because people don't go in and look at your resume and decide to go to be your friend. They don't go look at your resume when they say that they want to do business with you, they want to hear the stories of struggle and solutions search and then success that you have experienced. So the stories are so powerful and this is the true advanced way you build relationships with your clients and so when they know your story they feel attached to you and again this is a relationship builder this personality that is in your copy that is in your marketing system. This is where the relationship is built.

These stories can be your method of building very strong relationships with your clients because now they can relate to you on a deeper level and that's what marketing is all about.

Take the business from transactional to relational to become long term and way more powerful.

What message do you want to convey to your audience?

What is the story of struggle?

Describe the success in this story?

Tell your client how this relates to your business and the actions you want them to take.

Your story

Now, take your answers and tell your client a compelling story. Start with your struggle, your low point. Then move to your search for the solution, then move to your success and lead into your passion for this industry and how it relates to your client.

Example: This is my story for my electronic technician clients.

In 1994 I was stationed aboard the USS Carl Vinson, CVN70, a Nimitz class nuclear powered aircraft carrier. If you recall, the United States was smack dab in the middle of the first Gulf War. The Carl Vinson battle group was tasked with enforcing a no-fly zone over Iraq in support of our operations in Kuwait. We were in charge of making sure no foreign plane crossed the "Line of Death". This invisible line out in the desert was our sole responsibility and in order to make sure no planes crossed it we were flying planes 24/7 a nd in a heightened state of readiness. Well as luck would have it, we were sitting on watch in 2 plant at about 2am and with no warning at all the plant scrams. That means that it goes into a safety shutdown and we lose half the power on board the ship.

Now we weren't completely dead in the water, because 1 plant was fully operational and it is capable of supplying all the necessary steam to keep everything running. But the Captain was not too happy to be in such a predicament because if 1 plant experienced any power surges or if we needed to get anywhere in a hurry, we didn't have full capacity to do that. So we were made aware that no matter what it took we needed to get that plant up and running and FAST. So with a minimal investigation and an incident filed with Naval Reactors we were given permission to start back up, without knowing the exact cause of the scram. Not a great place to be in, given that we had no idea if this would happen again or not.

Well after about 32 hours of operation, guess what.... We went down again, but this time we had to find the cause of it. Now I would like you to imagine what it's like on board an aircraft carrier at sea standing still under the hot sun in the middle of summer with no ventilation, the captain breathing down your neck, the entire ship of 5500 blaming you on the predicament their in and you can't even come up with a reason as to why this is going on. Now that's pressure. We got the entire team of electronics technicians cracking on that problem, rank was of no importance, if someone had an idea then we looked at it. Now you may not be aware of it but the electronics inside a nuclear reactor 20 years ago was not microprocessor based, it was all solid state electronics, so there was no computer to help us diagnose the problem, it was up to the most experienced techs to troubleshoot the problem.

It took almost 40 hours of blood, sweat and tears but as I was waist deep inside an electronic cabinet enclosure I happened to look up above me and notice a very shiny object that was out of place, something just didn't look right, it was dangling above my head and everything should have been well connected and soldered down in there. I got someone to hand me a super bright flashlight and there it was, right inside the control rod drive electronics – a broken capacitor. There was a leg of the capacitor that had broken loose and was making partial contact with the circuit board. On occasion when we hit a big wave it would come out of circuit fully and then BAM, the plant scrams and we go in the dark. I was able to get a soldering iron in that tight spot and remove the capacitor; we just happened to have a replacement part on board the ship and when I compared the two parts I noticed there was a difference.

I was able to get a soldering iron in that tight spot and remove the capacitor; we just happened to have a replacement part on board the ship and when I compared the two parts I noticed there was a difference. The correct part that was supposed to be in the circuit had a much thicker lead; the broken part was much thinner. I replaced the capacitor with the mil-spec part (that's what we called the right part at the time) and we got back and operational. Now because of the politics behind nuclear power plants, especially those aboard Naval vessels there was a tremendous amount of investigation into the cause of this incident. Months later we got the official report of how that inferior part made it into our rod control system. It turns out that during the last operational upgrade we did a few months earlier that the contractor used a much less expensive part, remember our equipment is built by the cheapest bid. In an effort to save 32 cents they used a commercial grade capacitor instead of the military grade (mil spec) component. The only real differences between the two were that the military component could operate in a larger temperature range and it could endure higher levels of physical shock. Needless to say they made us change out every one of those commercial grade parts to make sure we never got into a mess like that again. A few years later after I did my time, I started my company called Power Control Services and we started repairing industrial electronic equipment. I vowed at that time to never skimp on a few cents worth of parts because I knew that in the long run, better parts make a better repair.

We have always used the best parts available and over the last 15 years we have improved upon that concept with things like our proactive rebuild process, our circuit board encapsulation method, IPC 7711/7721 Rework standards, ultrasonic cleaning process and many others...

What these improvements to our repairs has resulted in is not a repair at all, it is an equipment rebuild. A process we call our Platinum Level Rebuild Program.

This is a program unlike anything you will ever encounter and it is not available by anyone, anywhere except here at Power Control Services.

Example: This is my story for GKIC Marketer of the Year submission

My name is Walter Bergeron and this is my story with GKIC.

I began my company called Power Control Services in 1996 after I served in the United States Navy for 6 years as a Nuclear Reactor Operator, and yes I do glow in the dark in case you were wondering. My experience in the Navy led to an "entrepreneurial seizure" and in a 400 square foot shed I started repairing industrial electronics for the local manufacturing plants. Fast forward 15 years and now I have 2 repair centers, one in Broussard, Louisiana and the other in Atlanta, Georgia with over 40,000 square feet of building which makes us the largest national facility 100% dedicated to industrial electronic repairs. There are larger and there are higher volume facilities but they all do other things like sell new products and offer many other services, we focus only on repairs of electronic equipment. We also have 4 sales locations in Texas, Missouri, Nebraska and Georgia with outside sales staff manning those locations. We have had positive growth every year for the past 15 years and 2011 was our best year grossing $1.7 Million dollars in sales. We have a total staff of 15 employees with another 9 outside independent sales representatives.

I began to dabble in marketing in late 2010 with Magnetic Marketing, loving the ideas but never actually implementing anything of any real significance. 2011 came along and I got involved with Infusionsoft and actually implemented an email campaign. That's when I saw a glimmer of a result and it got me hooked. I made a commitment to attend the Fast Implementation Boot Camp, then I got my first phone call from Mr. Ron Penksa of GKIC and he opened my eyes a lot more with the Max Mentoring Program, which I enrolled into in September of 2011. I also made the trip to Chicago for the FAST Implementation Boot Camp, well at least that's what it said on the phone book in my hotel room but I never actually saw anything other than the inside of the hotel. I remember very vividly the exact moment that the light bulb went off in my head, the heavens opened up and the angels began to sing when Bill Glazer said to look around at my peers, that out of the person to my left and to my right and behind and in front of me that only one person would actually implement and take action on what he was there to preach to us. It was at that exact second that I decided that it would be ME! I knew it would be me because I had this same experience in the military.

You see, for the Nuclear Propulsion Program only 1 in 10 make it from start to finish and since I had made it through that program I knew I could make it through this one. So I went back to my hotel room and got to work, I worked through the entire night and got more marketing done in those few hours than I had gotten done all year long. I have thought about it a few times but I also remember talking to 2 of the guys that sat next to me at the FAST Implementation Boot Camp, 1 of them owned a furniture store with his brother and the other was launching a music education product that he made in his basement. Well the second day of the FAST Implementation Boot Camp I happened to look over at these 2 guys and the guy with the furniture store had left early, something more important to do I am sure. The other guy, the one with the educational product was actually asleep. Can you imagine that, Bill Glazer is on stage GIVING away secrets to marketing success, secrets to make our businesses a success and this guy is snoring away? I am sure he'll wake up and say to himself that this marketing crap doesn't work. I was certainly reassured at that point that I would be the one to make my marketing work, these two clowns certainly weren't going to do it.

When I returned to Louisiana I hit the ground running, I plastered a sign on my desk that I got from Tony Robbins that says "Take MASSIVE Action Today" and that's what I did. My Max Mentoring Coach Mr. Jeff Wright was giving me support as well as Ron Penksa kept me inspired with routine phone calls and words of encouragement, he even did an interview with me, very flattering. During the next 90 days I started 4 newsletters, wrote multiple long form sales letters with copy doodles all over them, sent out 3D mailers, raised our prices 15%, had my staff make me look like and idiot and a clown, fabricated an outrageous video sales case, recorded and implemented an automated webinar system, refined our USP and started 2 client membership programs, installed magnormous (bigger than enormous) signs outside the buildings, did multiple videos, revised our current marketing with deadlines and offers and stronger calls to action. In short, my business underwent a total transformation from an insignificant marketing system to multiple parallel projects of implementation.

That leaves me where I am today, still implementing every day, a member of the Lee Milteer Peak Performers Implementation Coaching Program and accepted into the Platinum Mastermind program. What a whirlwind the last few months have been. Thank you GKIC

Example: This is a picture I use for my story for GKIC Marketer of the Year submission

This is the picture taken at the September 2011 Fast Implementation Boot Camp. (See Figure 4.28) If you remember my story, the guy to my left was a struggling furniture store owner and he had left early. The guy to my right invented a music education product in his basement and had fallen asleep. Well look below to see what I was talking about.

Walter Bergeron
Marketer of the Year

Furniture store owner – or lack of one anyway. He left a few hours before the event was over. He had way more important things to do obviously.
NOT Marketer of the Year

Music education product inventor- woke up long enough to take the picture
NOT Marketer of the Year

Figure 4.28

Celebrity

Building celebrity into your marketing also adds credibility and exposure for you. To find them first you must begin to think locally and nationally about current and previous celebrities. These people are not necessarily involved in your industry, it just must be someone that your clients would think highly of and have respect for. I know many businesses that have a male clientele that loves football. So, in the fall every year they hire a retired NFL player, not a great player, but a well know player that lives locally and he comes out and signs autographs for their clients. This generates publicity as well as an event and adds credibility to the business.

You can also borrow celebrity status. Get pictures taken with a celebrity and then add a story behind it. At a recent event I was able to take a picture with Emmit Smith. I can put any kind of headline I want on an article and borrow the celebrity status of Emmit and it raises my own credibility. (See Figure 4.29)

You can use local celebrities that you haven't even met, especially if they are well known. I live about 50 miles from where Discovery Channel Sons of Guns is filmed. So I used them as a local celebrity them when I speak to audiences like mine that like guns and southern drama. They don't fit in with my hobbies but my clients loved this show, so I borrowed that celebrity and used it to my benefit and you can do the same thing for your business too. (See Figure 4.30)

Now when most people think of a celebrity they think of a person, well you can go beyond that as well. In my industrial repair business I used a national celebrity company and this carries tremendous clout with our other clients. So we didn't limit ourselves to finding famous people, although we did that too!

Companies – be careful of copyright laws here, many companies are very sensitive and restrictive on use of their logos and registered trademarks, consulting with an attorney is highly advised.

(See Figure 4.31)

Where could you find your own celebrity?

❑ What contacts with a celebrity company do you have?

❑ Do any companies endorse you or do you represent any companies?

❑ Do you have any connections to a local celebrity? Any events you can attend where they will be?

Emmitt Smith works well with any football fan

Figure 4.29

Barbara Corcoran works well with any entrepreneur or fan of "Shark Tank"

Adam West works well with baby boomers and science fiction fans

Figure 4.30

Figure 4.31

Continuity Programs
(Contractor's Service Agreements)

These are programs where your clients pay you an ongoing fee whether they use your services or not. Sometimes referred to as residual income but with a little creativity, continuity income and programs can be added to any type of business. I never thought it would work for my industry of electronic repairs but if you look at the examples I provided you will see that I was able to put continuity into industrial electronic repairs. Not an industry accustomed to monthly recurring charges, I must tell you.

Here are some ways you can introduce or expand monthly paid continuity into your business.

> **Priority services** – Membership levels would each get better and better services as they ascend up your ladder of membership. Bronze, Silver and Gold levels each get better and better services each time they do business with you.

> **Rush services** – Myself, I used differing times we would repair equipment in. Bronze was 10 working days, Silver was 5 working days and Gold was 24 hour service

> **Head of the line** – This one is used by Disney parks to their great benefit, think of ways to add this service to your client's experience and charge them for this privilege.

> **Special events** – This is for clients at different levels or if you already hold events have special areas for your best clients. GKIC does a great job by having an area with food, drinks and comfortable seating for its Diamond level members at all of their events.

> **Special monthly coaching** – If there is ongoing monthly contact you wish to establish, have monthly coaching calls or monthly visits to your office to get special education or training.

> **Membership websites** – Create evergreen content and offer monthly paid access to this special training. This can be combined very easily with monthly coaching by recording the monthly coaching and putting it up on a website and making it available to all clients for a fee.

There are so many ways to add continuity into your business model, it just takes a little creativity and you'll be surprised just how much your clients are craving more attention from you.

Some of my own examples I used in the industrial repair industry: (See Figures 4.32 and 4.33)

> Memberships - Create continuity income as well as give clients levels to aspire to and attain more of your products and services. The way we created them was to take the best of our services and bundle them into a package and offer it as a membership. We chose levels based on the services and then developed the marketing pieces.

> **Platinum Rebuild Program** - This is our highest level of service and takes the best of everything we have to offer and rolls it into one neat monthly program with a fee paid on the front end. After a few months of selling this service we realized that it was easy to sell and so we are currently considering a higher Titanium level. We started with what we could implement quickly and easily, but now with a little planning we will have an even higher level to build our services to and a fee to match that level of service.

> **Gold Repair Program** - You might notice that we used ZERO creativity when naming our memberships, no need to reinvent the wheel. Clients are accustomed to hearing these types of membership levels so we just played into what they have heard before. This membership level is one of our lowest levels of service and substantially different from our

Platinum level so it is easy to upsell clients to
Platinum

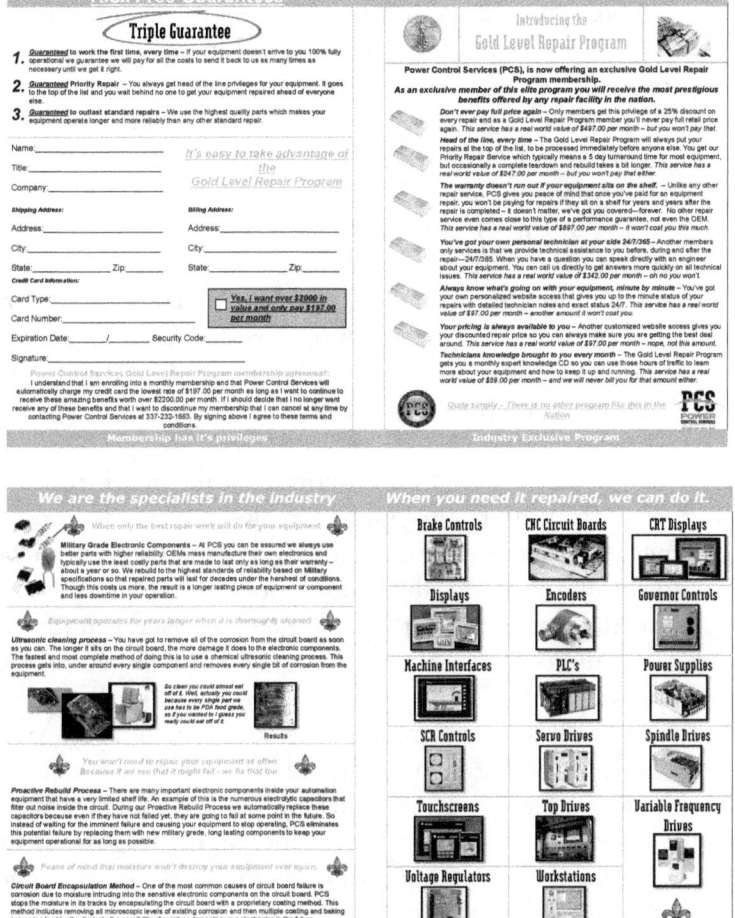

Figure 4.32

Innovation

New products and services – to existing clients

You must continually develop and implement new products and services for your clients. This may take the form of entirely new lines of products (like Solar Panels, Generators, Tankless Water Heaters, Duct Sealing, Smart Thermostats) or entirely new services you offer. It may also take the form of continuity programs or creating packages and bundles of products or services in new packages and ways of presenting it to your clients that makes it new to them. You need to keep things fresh and new so they will always have reasons to remain as current clients of yours and not stray from your herd.

Areas to look at constant innovation:

Continuity programs – really easy to do most of the time with a little creativity and you'll truly stand out because most industries do this very poorly. Any of the previous marketing programs, they all need constant updating and attention to keep them fresh and make sure they get improved ROI.

Seek out examples outside your industry of what's working in regards to marketing. Earlier we talked about signage and when I saw what the casino industry was doing with sequential signs on the side of the highway, multiple sequential signs that allowed them to develop longer and larger more elaborate messages. I applied that idea to my own business but this idea came from the casino industry and I applied it to industrial repairs.

Don't follow along with what everyone else is doing in your industry, 99% of them are wrong. Become the leader, you will not be appointed the leader, you must take that title and own it for yourself by claiming it and taking the road less traveled.

Become a student of marketing and of your entire industry. That includes your competitors as well. Look at all the marketing that is going on inside and outside of your own industry and even become a client of your own competitor. Now this may be a sticking point for many people, there is a desire not to help your competitors by doing business with them. Instead, think of this as research and development. You want to know what your clients are getting from your competitors in terms of marketing. You want to know how your competitors stack up against yourself, you want to know what it feels like to be a client of your competitor and then you can compare that to being a client of yours. If they are doing a better job or if you feel better after the work completed by your competitor then you need to step up your marketing game. But, if you see that they are doing a really poor job or you can see the big holes in their marketing system, then you know that you can continue to build on your own and get better and better and pull away from your competitors.

Become a reader of books about all subjects inside and outside of your industry. Be thirsty for new knowledge about marketing and about subjects inside and outside of your own industry. Attend industry trade shows like Comfortech or even just local events put on by associations like Service Roundtable or ACCA. I am always amazed by the small percentage of contractors who set aside time to attend trade shows outside their immediate area. This will be one of the areas you want to be very knowledgeable of when it comes time to look for other companies to purchase. If you are a great student and thirsty for knowledge about the products and services that closely relate to your business as well as businesses that are complementary to your business, then you will be a whole lot more knowledgeable when it comes time find other companies to purchase. If you don't have the time needed to attend industry trade shows in industries you are interested in, at least join association in that industry so you begin receiving information on the products and services that your potential acquisition sells. You will know which ones will tie-in better to your own company so that you could merge with and build your own empire.

Example

An example of this comes from my client Wade. Now Wade's primary business is air conditioning. Just like many of you, he repairs air conditioning systems in people's houses, which as you can imagine in south Louisiana in the middle of August at 95 degrees and 80% humidity for 5 months out of the year is pretty big business. But come October, when the fall weather hits us and the temperature gets to 70 degrees, air conditioning business drops to almost nothing. So Wade needed something to keep his business afloat during the winter. So as an astute and driven entrepreneur Wade asked his clients what they needed done in the winter months and many of them told him they do kitchen remodeling work during the winter. Now he knew nothing about kitchen remodeling but it didn't matter because that's what his clients wanted. So he went out and contracted a well-known kitchen remodeling company and he sold the services to his clients with a nice mark up. His clients loved it because they already had a valued and trusted relationship with Wade's air conditioning company and so Wade was able to sell enough kitchen remodeling jobs to help him make it through the winters profitably. So he started doing kitchen remodeling as an upsell to his air conditioning services. This is a way to take advantage of innovation to increase sales to his business and avoid negative profit months by simply solving a problem for his clients. This was also a way for him to test drive another business for a possible strategic acquisition. He made sure this was a good fit first by sub-contracting out the work and then, if it met his needs, he could look at buying a kitchen remodeling business to exponentially grow his business.

Trend Watching

This is how you avoid being a victim of your own success, get rid of the blinders and become aware of your surroundings. Don't become the next Blockbuster Video or Circuit City or Betamax, if you're old enough to remember that. Right now you see companies like Radio Shack desperately trying to reinvent themselves, but it could have been avoided if they had made themselves aware of what's going on around them more quickly.

- ➢ **Clients** – Constant feedback from them is crucial, don't ignore complaints.
- ➢ **Technology** – Embrace it don't fight against it.
- ➢ **Competitors** – Become a client of your competitors to see how they treat their own clients and how they market to them.
- ➢ **Economy** – This one can be very tough to not get depressed or deeply involved in, remember, as you get involved that you are an entrepreneur and you control your own micro economy. Make yourself aware of ways to prosper no matter what the economy is doing.
- ➢ **Politics** – This is the same as the economy. Also, your business is not the forum for you to voice your political opinions in. Not normally anyway.
- ➢ **Financial** – What are the financial conditions of your industry, your clients, yourself? Be aware and take advantage of opportunities no matter what the financials are like for your clients. When they are tight on cash you could introduce new cost saving efforts, when they are flush with cash you can introduce new premium services. Being aware of what's going on is of tremendous value to you.

An easy way to get more information from your clients is to use surveys every other month to ask them their thoughts in these areas of their business. Survey monkey has some great tools to use for this.

Are you ready to take the next logical step? Schedule your contractor market assessment. So you can identify the prospects that are 600 X more likely to turn into a new customer…and it's FREE too! Simply go to www. MEERScore.com/freeoffer and fill out the application for a 45 minute phone call with Mike Layton.

As a special bonus, this includes an additional FREE strategy session to get your customized plan for exponential growth with Walter Bergeron.

Chapter 5

Running On Autopilot

Do It On Purpose

Had I not had all major systems in my business documented I would have never been able to sell one of my businesses for $10million. Actually I would not have been able to sell it at all. Of the many things that buyers require when making a purchase of this size is a well-documented and proven system to run the business. There needs to be processes in place and people to manage the processes but all of this cannot simply be in your head, you must document it all to be able to pass on the business to a buyer.

Last winter I took in one of my boats for its' winterization service, yeah I know it's probably a made up service these guys used to sell me a 3 year contract for my boat but I buy it and a couple times a year I take it in and get a bunch of work done. A few months ago I called the dealership and the nice young lady Samantha answers the phone and takes all my information, make model, what service I need done and then a few days later haul the boat over to the dealership. Now, as I pulled up to the service department at the dealership a guy walks out with a clipboard and walks up to my truck so I roll down the window and he greets me by name. He says good morning Mr. Bergeron and then he goes over everything I wanted done to the boat. I sign the ticket, he directs me where to park the boat and I am on my way in 10 minutes. So none of this happened on accident. When I scheduled my appointment they got my name and boat make, model and color so when I pulled in, he could easily identify who I was and he got the right ticket and put it on the clipboard and walked out to greet me, it was great. So during the winter the boat sat in storage and then a couple of weeks ago we are heading to our lake house so I want to take the boat. So I call the dealership and schedule its' de-winterization appointment. (Quit laughing at me I know it's probably made up and I'm being taken for a ride, but I bought the service and at this point I've had great experiences at this dealership) So when I called to schedule the appointment and of course Samantha takes all my information, she asks me the same intake questions, name, make model, what I want done. It all seems like I am ready to have another quick drop off and great service. So I hook up the boat to my truck and haul the boat all the way over there, but this time it's different. The parking lot is filled with boats attached to trucks parked in every damn direction really haphazardly and so I have to invent a new place and park partly in the grass and partly on the pavement. I park my truck and boat, I gotta' now get out of the truck walk into the dealership through the showroom to the back of the dealership to the service counter, wait in line then I tell them who I am and of course they can't find the paperwork (yep paperwork, not yet sophisticated enough to have the damn appointment on a computer yet I guess) so I go through name, make, model, what I need done all over again. Then I go out and wait for the minion to come out and tell me where to park the boat, but of course there's only 1 guy so he's got to finish taking in all the boats so I wait until he gets all his paperwork done before he comes out to direct traffic of me and all the other guys with boats for service for the day. So, I am there for over an hour. And I know this sounds frustrating but that's not the real problem because this guy tells me more than once that he's new and that I should for some reason forgive him for making such a damn mess of things because he's still trying to figure out how in the world he's going to eventually get things organized. And the point of this is that it's completely evident that last winter the experience I had was an accident, the guy running it had been there for years and he slowly developed a system, but he never wrote a bit of it down, no documentation and when he

> In businesses without documented system, everything happens by accident. Both the good things and the bad and the worst part is that as a company there is no memory of how things are done when employees leave. This is a failure to have a business that is people dependent and not systems dependent.

left and the new guy started he had to start from scratch because there was nothing passed on to him, no process, no procedures, no documented systems of any kind. I can only imagine how bad things are going to get if that poor girl Samantha that answers the phone ever leaves, I imagine the new girl will have to invent what questions to ask me when I call in for an appointment.

Not only will you need these systems in place to make your business eligible to be purchased but as part of these blueprints you are going to learn how to buy other companies. Just like the boat dealership I just spoke about, many companies have poorly documented if not non-existent business system documentation and therefore many of their processes are not done consistently. So with a full set of properly documented systems you can much more easily take an underperforming company with poorly documented systems and turn it into an much more profitable asset for you and then be able to use that business to grow your current business' sales and market share and build your empire. If you want to buy an underperforming boat dealership give me a call. All you need is a consistent service process and this thing might be a goldmine for you.

So let's get into it. In a very real way, your strategy for building your systems *is* your business strategy and the business systems you put in place *are* your business.

Keep in mind the idea of the "franchise prototype," the idea that you should create your business as if you were going to replicate it "5,000 times." The idea that, if you do it right, that your business will run itself systematically, predictably, flawlessly. The idea that **systems dependency works and people dependency** doesn't. The idea that systems rather than dehumanizing your people, actually free them to do the work that matters. Now we know this isn't anything you haven't heard before. Contractor associations like Success Group International, NexStar, Service Roundtable, PSI, AT500 and others have been a source for documented contractor processes for years. If you ever plan on selling your business at its full value you will need to do more than point to bunch of someone else's binders on your shelf. Thousands of contractors could do that. You need to document and implement the processes or systems that you use in YOUR business. That's the only way you can sell it and walk away OR it's the only way that you can keep your business and spend worry-free time away from the business.

Also keep in mind that systems are dynamic. Your business is an organism and, like living organisms, it grows and changes with time and experience. You don't simply put a system in place, then expect it to run forever. It won't run forever. It will become obsolete as your markets change, your business grows, and Murphy's Law ("if anything *can* go wrong, it *will* go wrong") is alive and well.

Systems ignored become bottlenecks. Also, keep in mind the idea that the systems of your business are *integrated*. One system links to another, the output from one system is the input to another, and changes to one system impact all the systems "downstream" from it. So when Samantha takes my name and make and model of my boat that output of her system is the input to the service department, or at least it should be anyway. The result when all things are operating properly is Synergy. Meaning that this system, when operating smoothly and profitably, is greater than the sum of its' parts. Your business is much more than the sum of its parts. You'd be amazed at home many contractors don't have fundamental systems like accounting integrated with their dispatch systems. Even many large successful contractors lose access to years of historical customer data when they migrate from an older accounting, or dispatch system to the latest product from a new supplier. If they needed to sell their business, how do you think prospective buyers would value this lack of information. If you were buying a business without five years of clean information, how would you value it? I bet you'd pay less for it. Or it should be.

A System Has A Purpose

A system has a purpose and produces a result. And an effective system produces an exact result you intend it to produce, and it does so like clockwork, predictably, on time, on budget, every time. Reliability is the hallmark of an effective system. When all your systems are working reliably to produce their intended results, and they are integrated with each other, then your business operates reliably. A system is either intentional or accidental. Either you intentionally developed and installed the system, or it simply "happened" as the random result of the activities of your people. Is there any doubt which option is better? Which approach leads to consistently effective systems? Which approach results in a business that works?

The point is that you should proactively create your systems, not merely let them happen randomly. And every system should have a specific purpose, a result it is responsible for producing.

Don't treat systems design as an academic exercise. It's real world. Do your system design work on the spot. Do it on the shop floor, in the kitchen, in the showroom, on the road, at the assembly line, on the trucks, at the drill press, at the telephone. Be where the work gets done and see what's happening and what needs to happen. Involve the people who do the work.

The biggest roadblock at this point is that many entrepreneurs get overwhelmed with all that needs to be done to create and document all of their systems. So let me help you, let me give you a process to create the type of system that will be a tremendous asset.

Setting up a Massive Action work environment

Set aside time each week for your implementation homework, you must make an appointment with yourself or with your team to make sure this time gets set aside. If you are completing these exercises with a team set aside time for each of you to work independently and then time for you to work together on creating a shared vision.

- ❑ Find a quiet room where you won't be disturbed
- ❑ Put a Do Not Disturb sign on the door, then close it and lock it
- ❑ Put phone on do not disturb or just unplug it
- ❑ Turn off you cell phone
- ❑ Turn off your email
- ❑ Turn off any instant messaging or chat features
- ❑ Close out of all programs except the one you are using to complete this exercise

- ✓ *Take Massive Action Every Day*
- ✓ *Good Is Good Enough*
- ✓ *Simultaneous Implementation*

By using these 3 philosophies you will make your implementation happen faster than it has ever happened before

A Quick Story

This may seem irrelevant but follow me on this. I was born on Halloween, yep October 31st, and so this holiday has always meant a great deal to me. I dress up in a costume every year, and yes even now I dress up and we throw a BIG Halloween/Birthday party. Over the years my wife has taken this to a whole new level. We now go shopping in August and start to prepare for the big party. She has accumulated 10 pallets, yes 10 forklift sized pallets of Halloween decorations. 6 foot wide by 6 foot tall by 8 foot high pallets of every imaginable Halloween decoration including 8 life sized animated horror movie props. One of those animated props is Michael Meyers, of the famed Halloween movies. So, back to my massive action story.

Hockey mask on and knife in hand, I placed Michael Meyers just outside my office door with those signs taped all over him to "STAY AWAY", "OWNER BITES REALLY HARD" and wouldn't you know it, it worked again. Everyone left me alone so I could continue my trek into marketing implementation.

I also realized that 5 days a week was not enough, even during the weekends my mind would be racing with ideas and enthusiasm about the marketing ideas from the week. I would wake up on Saturday mornings with these thoughts, but by Monday they would be gone. So I took massive action again and started waking up an hour earlier than the rest of the household, sit at my laptop with a cup of "Joe" and I would write sales letters, and make revisions to copy and sometimes just THINK. In the peace of the early morning before the sun had come up I would just think and dream of what I am accomplishing and make it real in my mind, that the reality of success had already happened and I was living the life I imagined. And then I would get right back at it with an all new vigor.

So if you ever have an excuse that your staff won't leave you alone or you just can't find the time. You just need to dig a little deeper and find a more creative and totally extreme way to MAKE that time. MAKE it happen. MAKE it massive every single day.

I decided that "The third time is a charm" would be my good is good enough measuring stick or mantra. I would work on something and give myself 3 revisions, then I would send it out the door to my clients. If I couldn't make it perfect after 3 tries, then so be it, errors and all were going out the door and I would just have to make corrections after the fact, when and if they ever were needed.

This part of my philosophy seems to defy physics, you can only do one thing at a time. You can only be in one place at a time and it is physically impossible to do anything other than one thing at a time. Well, that is in essence a correct assumption but what I wanted to do was to get a task completed up to a point that I could simply go no further. What that meant to me was for example…

When I started my newsletters.

I would do as much as I could as fast as I could and then I would hit a roadblock. Sometimes I would simply run out of ideas, sometimes my eyes would start to cross because I had been staring at the computer screen far too long or sometimes I just got bored with what I was doing. So I would then stop go take care of something in the office, or put stamps on envelopes or go fold some long form sales letters or some other task that would move me forward, onto something that gave me more satisfaction and that I could make more progress on. I would come back to the newsletters after a couple of hours and finish them up but at the end of the day I had two or three implemented strategies and that made multiple things happen at the same time. I did this every day and then as different projects took different timeframes to complete after a couple of weeks it was like every day something new was being completed and getting fully implemented. That fueled my enthusiasm so I worked even harder to make that happen again.

How do you start? There's an infinite variety of ways you can approach systemization, and different businesses require different systems. There are some systems common to all businesses, although even these have variations on the common theme (for instance an income statement is an information system common to all businesses, yet there is an unlimited variety of ways to prepare and present even this most common of information systems).

So you are going to start with the "big picture" of your business as a whole, and work your way through systems, sub-systems, and sub-sub-systems until you reach the point where further systemization becomes an exercise in the trivial. Then you stop. For instance, you will certainly need a system for recruiting and hiring employees, but you almost certainly will not need a system for sorting paper clips by size and color. That's trivial and ridiculous.

Sometimes, when in a developmental situation or when innovating products and services and the new systems to produce them, you may not be able to be as precise as you would like. After all, if it's a new idea, a new way of doing things, a new product, you may not know *exactly* what is possible and exactly what you can produce. You'll be using the system itself as a way to refine what is possible. It's a legitimate use of trial and error.

Systems Documentation Process

To properly and completely document an existing business process or procedure so that it can be used for ongoing operations as well as employee training.

1. Specify the name of the system. Give the system a brief, descriptive name and a code number if you like. The code number will help you with identifying the procedure in your systems manual when you get many of them. Just like the name of this one is called the Systems Documentation Process and if you give it a number such as 1.1 and this series of documents that start with 1 will always be about documentation procedures. Then anything starting with 2 could be another series like all Leadership documents, and anything with 3 could be Money systems. Just use a logical way to keep things well organized.

2. Specify the result of the system. Write a clear concise statement of the result the system is intended to accomplish. Nothing too fancy, just what you want this system to accomplish.

3. Diagram the system. Diagram the steps in the system showing their sequence and how they relate to each other. Use a simple box and arrow diagram with brief captions to describe each step. I like to use powerpoint but there are lots of other ways to diagram the system, just use a software that you can easily make changes to because your system will change and you want to be able to easily and quickly make changes yourself.

4. Describe system steps in clearly-stated benchmarks. Each box in your system diagram is actually a work step, an action. When you identify each action in sequence, you're creating the benchmarks that make the process clear and unmistakable to anyone who will perform the work or supervise it. So in this step, you take each box in your systems diagram and restate the work in a complete sentence that clearly communicates exactly the work or action to be taken. (See Figures 5.1, 5.2 and 5.3)

5. Assign accountabilities. Identify by position, not by person, who will be accountable for the system as a whole and who will be accountable for each of its benchmarks. When you finish documenting the system, a copy of the systems action plan will go into the operating manual of each person in those positions.

6. Determine the timing. Knowing when each benchmark needs to be performed is a key element of getting the result you want. Establish the timing for each step, certain steps only, or for the system as a whole, as appropriate. This might be in terms of clock time (by 10 a.m.), project time (day 1, day 4), generic phrases (upon receipt, weekly), or a combination of these.

7. Identify required resources. Every system requires resources of the following types: staffing, work space, facilities, equipment, supplies, and information. Make a detailed listing of the specific resources and quantities of each needed to operate the system, as appropriate. Some systems won't have a lengthy list of resources; it may be just the individuals involved and their "everyday" work supplies.

➢ **Staffing** – The amount and types of manpower needed to operate the system such as how many people, what positions, what skills they need, how many hours, particular shifts, schedules, backups if important to your situation.

➢ **Workspace and facilities** – Amount of space needed like square footage or configuration, the types of space needed, the layout, efficient placement of equipment or utilities, environmental conditions.

> **Equipment**- like machinery, tools, furniture, office equipment, vehicles, instruments, etc..
> **Supplies** – Consumables like office supplies, raw materials, ingredients, components, forms, paperwork, etc..
> **Information** – databases, pricing sheets, subscriptions, instructions, reference materials like other procedures, etc..

8. Determine how you will quantify the system. How will you know if you are getting the result you want from your system? How can you make decisions about your business without objective information about the performance of your systems? You need quantification to give you that objective view. Without it, you're shooting in the dark. The best time to create the method for quantifying each system is at the time you design and document it. Take some time in the design and documentation stage to think about how you will quantify the system. In other words, how will you objectively determine whether the system, as it's operating in your business, is giving you the result it's supposed to. This little bit of extra time spent now will pay you back in big dividends later. Starting to measure your systems' effectiveness early on, establishing a baseline for comparison, will put you ahead of the game in your efforts to have good, reliable, useful information - management information.

9. Establish standards. Set the standards for performance of the system and behavior of the staff operating the system. Standards are most easily stated in terms of: quantity, quality, and behavior. These could include measures of output, defects,
cost per item, guidelines for staff behavior, dress codes, and even ethical standards. If it is key to producing a successful result, then you 'll need to set standards for it. Standards determine how well, or how poorly, your business systems accomplish their purposes. Standards answer questions like:

How well? How much? How many? How fast? How attractive? How safe? How clean? How simple (or complex)? How helpful? How honest? How hot (or cold)? How cost-effective?

10. Document the system. Put it in writing. The format we recommend for documenting your systems is called a "systems action plan." You can use the worksheets in this blueprint, or a format of your own design, but *do* put it in writing. It's not done until it's documented. Documentation forces you to think through the system thoroughly. It eliminates errors due to imperfect memory and reduces the likelihood that unproductive habits will creep into the system. A documented system is easy to learn, and learn the right way. Otherwise, you just have another form of people dependency rather than system dependency. The best way to document systems in your company is to have a consistent format that everyone can understand and use. Now don't get overwhelmed because there are many ways to quickly and easily document your systems.

11. Write an outline of the system. Give the system a brief, descriptive outline in a written format to give you a place to start for writing your action plan. This gives you a structure to build your procedure on. This isn't always necessary but it can be very helpful when the systems are long and complex and have many parts to them and interactions between other steps.

12. Write out all details of the system. Write a clear concise detailed description of how you perform the tasks with given the system is intended to accomplish. If you look at the examples you can see that there is a lot of detail in some of the steps. The steps are detailed enough to eliminate any confusion, that's not to say that they eliminate complexity. In the procedure steps you need the right level of complexity to make sure the task gets done correctly versus simplicity where the steps can be open for interpretation.

13. Complete the Action Plan. Complete the action plan that includes all the details from previous steps, the timing, the accountabilities, the results, the benchmarks, the resources, quantification and standards. These can be multiple pages such as in the example I provided. There is not typical length of a process, it takes as long as it takes to get it right. Take your time and get it right the first time.

14. Keep all documents in your Systems Manuals. Each action plan needs a place to reside and your physical copy goes into your Systems Manual or you may call it your Operations Manual. Each workspace should have a copy of the action plan that applies to the job functions they perform. This way if an employee can perform multiple functions then at each work space that person goes to they can perform that job and have access to the action plans that apply. This can be especially helpful when an employee steps in to fill in temporarily, the procedure is a fresh reminder of what to do. Make sure you also have an electronic copy to put onto your membership site for on the job training.

15. Determine type of actions of the system. Identify what type of system you are going to be documenting to determine if you need to simply do an audio recording or that you need to do a video. This comes to a question of whether or not there is any demonstrable task or not. If it involves computer work, then this it a demonstration. If there are physical tasks then this is demonstration. If there is simply information only, like a key concept, then this is suitable for the information only type of audio recording.

16. Information based procedure. Many of the leadership procedures which are key conceptual procedures will be covered with this type of documentation.

17. Audio recordings. There are many ways to record an audio information procedure. Using a headset and your computer, a handheld voice recorder or record a phone conversation. Then transfer the audio to both a CD and electronic MP3 format.

18. Automobile University. Give the audio CD's to employees for training to and from work or at work or any time that listening to them will be convenient. A way to make sure they listen and a way to incentivize training is to record a key word into the audio and weekly give prizes for whoever can tell you the key word in the audio.

19. Demonstration based procedure. Any type of task that is able to be video recorded to enhance training and documentation of the system is perfectly suitable for video.

20. Demonstration Type. If the task has anything to do with your computer then you will need to use screen capture software to record this task. Any task that has any physical activity is a demonstration type of activity.

21. Computer Based Procedures. There are many screen capture software available, the most popular are Camtasia and Screen Flow which are both very capable of recording activities involving use of your computer. They also have the added benefit of being able to edit out any unwanted um's and ah's or just plain mistakes in your video.

22. Screen Capture. When capturing the tasks taking place on the computer screen make sure you record your voice to give instructions as you use the computer for the task you are recording. The voice recording can also be transcribed into an editable document, which can also give you a head start with the written documentation of your process.

---

23. Training Website. You will want to place all of your documented procedures in a centralized location so that you can have your employees view it from may locations or just to have a convenient place to store all of this media. I myself have had much of our data, procedures and video training used at first on our local server, then when we began to open multiple locations across the nation that didn't work. So I began to use Kajabi and then Customerhub. Now if you are not familiar with this type of website it is simply a website that you own that allows you to upload any and all of your procedures including written documentation, audio and video files. It also allows you to control access and have different levels of access. There were some procedures which were only for management staff such as how to terminate and employee, which I didn't want everyone to have access to. These membership sites allowed me to give specific people and positions control over what content they could access.

24. Physical Tasks. Any time a task requires an employee taking an action other than strictly using the computer, then this is an ideal time to use Direct To Camera type of video recordings.

25. Video Recording. Record your videos in any way you can, many smart phones can easily record video on good enough quality to use for recording procedures. You can use web cams or purchase an HD video camera to make high quality video. Keep in mind that video is important but don't forget to get great audio when you do video recording as well. Many times the audio in the video recordings is neglected, but the audience will forgive bad video well before they will forgive bad audio. Spend some time and get the audio right when you record video.

26. On The Job Training. Use your procedures for frequent employee training. This is also a great format to train new employees and get them up to speed very quickly. This is one way the time and effort in creating these systems will begin to pay for itself in the time saved training without documented systems. Formatting your processes and procedures in a way that is convenient for your employees to absorb information is also crucial. Such as the MP3 format for audio the MP4 format for video the DVDs for video more on their computer.

In my previous example at the boat dealership had the new employee been able to train himself using previously documented processes and procedures I would've had a great experience every time I frequented this business. This would've saved the business substantial cost in training the new employee not to mention the savings of not losing current clients. That would've been a seamless transition from the old employees to the new employees.

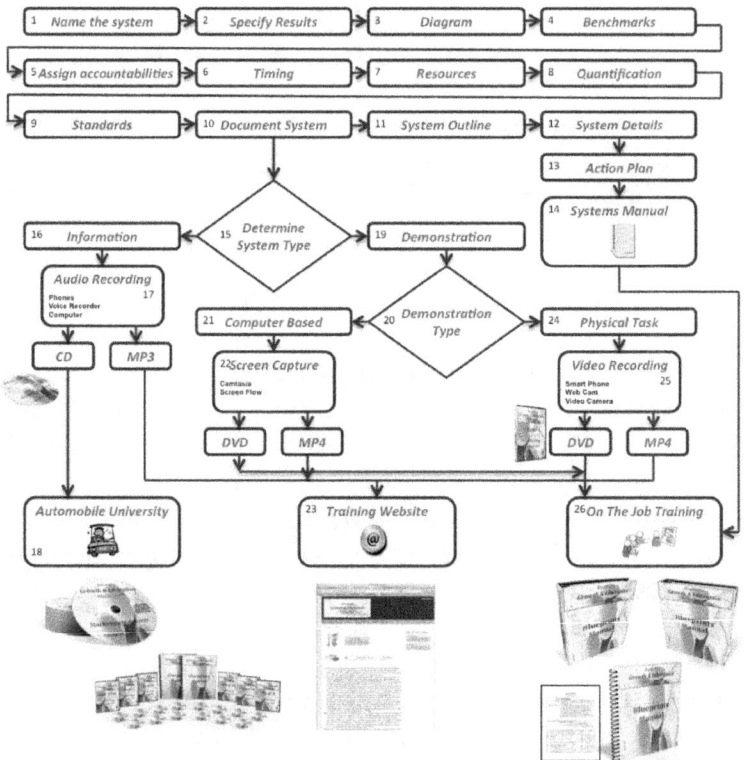

Figure 5.1

System Diagram
Repair Log-in

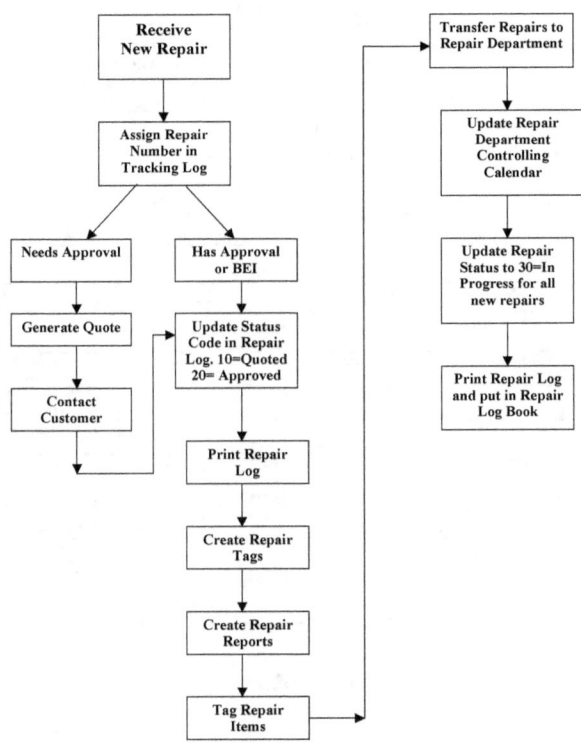

Figure 5.2

ACTION PLAN
Document1
Ver. 2/1/02 3:16 PM

TITLE:	**Logging In Repairs**
RESULT:	To quickly and efficiently track repairs until returned to customer.
LOGIC:	Customer Satisfaction and Company Work Flow are dependent upon all repairs being accurately tracked through each stage of the repair process-from login to shipping.
MATERIALS NEEDED:	Network Computer, **Repair Tracking Log book** (binder with excel doc. C:/My Documents.Excel Files.Repair Log.xls), Tracking Tag (4 3/4" X 2 3/8" Manila/Strung Shipping Tag)., **Repair Label** (Avery # 6490,Word Doc. C:/My Documents.Power Control Services.Labels.Repair Label Template), **Repair Status Label** (Avery # 6490,Word Doc. C:/My Documents.Power Control Services.Labels.Repair Status Label Template), **Electronic repair report** (Word Doc. i.e. C:/My Documents.Repair Reports.August Repairs), Green Highlighter, **Quick Books for Quotes, Fax Cover Sheet** (C:/My Documents.Power Control Services.Fax Documents), and a list of repair status codes.

POSITION WITH OVERALL ACCOUNTABILITY:	Tracking Clerk
REPORTING POSITIONS:	Shipping and Receiving Department Supervisor, Branch Manager
STAFF POSITIONS:	Shipping Receiving Clerk, Accounting Clerk, Bench Technician, S&R Supervisor

#	ACTION ITEMS TO BE COMPLETED	DONE BY	DUE BY
1.	Receive a new repair. Gather all customer supplied information and paperclip together. See Receiving Packages System.	Shipping and Receiving Clerk	As received
2.0	To Login Repairs: Open **Repair Log.** (File My Documents.Excel Files.Repair Log.)	Tracking Clerk	Completed by the Next business Day
2.0.1	Open Excel.	Tracking Clerk	Completed by the Next business Day
2.0.2	Click on File. Click on Open.	Tracking Clerk	Completed by the Next business Day
2.0.3	A smaller screen will pop up. At the top you will see the words "Look In:" You want to look in C:/MY DOCUMENTS. You may need to Click on the up arrow to find all the Folders in C:/.	Tracking Clerk	Completed by the Next business Day
2.0.4	Double Click on the My Documents Folder. This brings up the contents of My Documents.	Tracking Clerk	Completed by the Next business Day
2.0.5	Double click on the Excel Files Folder. This brings up the contents of Excel Files.	Tracking Clerk	Completed by the Next business Day
2.0.6	Double click on the file Repair Log. This will open the **Repair Log** Spreadsheet.	Tracking Clerk	Completed by the Next business Day
2.1	Update the Rev. date to today's date on every page.	Tracking	Completed by the

Figure 5.3

This method is one of the many ways to document your business systems. Now this format focuses on making sure that the processes and procedures are documented correctly. This is not a quick one-hour tutorial to get you to be able to document a process or procedure in only five minutes. You will spend some time to get this right. You will have to inject a certain level of complexity to get this done correctly. This is not necessarily about simplicity are speed this is about accuracy and long-term operation of your business. You will have to spend some time and puts more effort into this knowing that even with all the time and effort but in you will have to edit it at some point. Remember you'll be using the processes and procedures when you go to buy and sell other companies and so is critically important to make sure that their correct the first time.

Business Systems

Although there are variations to this rule, there are fundamental systems common to all businesses, common foundational areas that must be systematized and documented to keep a business running at it's optimum level. These systems are Leadership Systems, Management Systems, Money Systems, Marketing Systems, Sales Systems and Production Systems. (See Figure 5.4) Each one of these sets of systems has a very specific function within every business as well as a very specific set of sub-systems that operate and integrate with the other sets of systems.

If you recall my two experiences when I went to have my boat serviced. The first time I went I had a great experience, all of the systems seemed to be operating and integrated with each other. The girl that answered the phone took all of my information and it must have been integrated with the service department because they knew my name before I told them upon my arrival. They knew what I needed done and gave me great instructions and handled all of my needs with precision and professionalism. There seemed to be some type of systems dependent operation at work, though I was later to find out that it failed because there was no documentation of these systems. My second experience was terrible. The integration wasn't there and things were being run as a people dependent operation and the people were failing. No systems, no documentation, they were miserable and I was miserable. Not the way to do business. So let's see what they should have done.

On the next page you find a systems diagram that shows your business in the center as well as all six areas of systematization that you need to have which we'll discuss. They all feed into your business. In the last section we talked about the systems documentation process and that really is what you business is, it's your operations manual, it's your employee training, the automobile University that we spoke about, it is your daily operations. On a large scale these are the tools you're going to use to buy other businesses as well

---

as the asset you're going to use to sell your business to get you to your daily liberation.

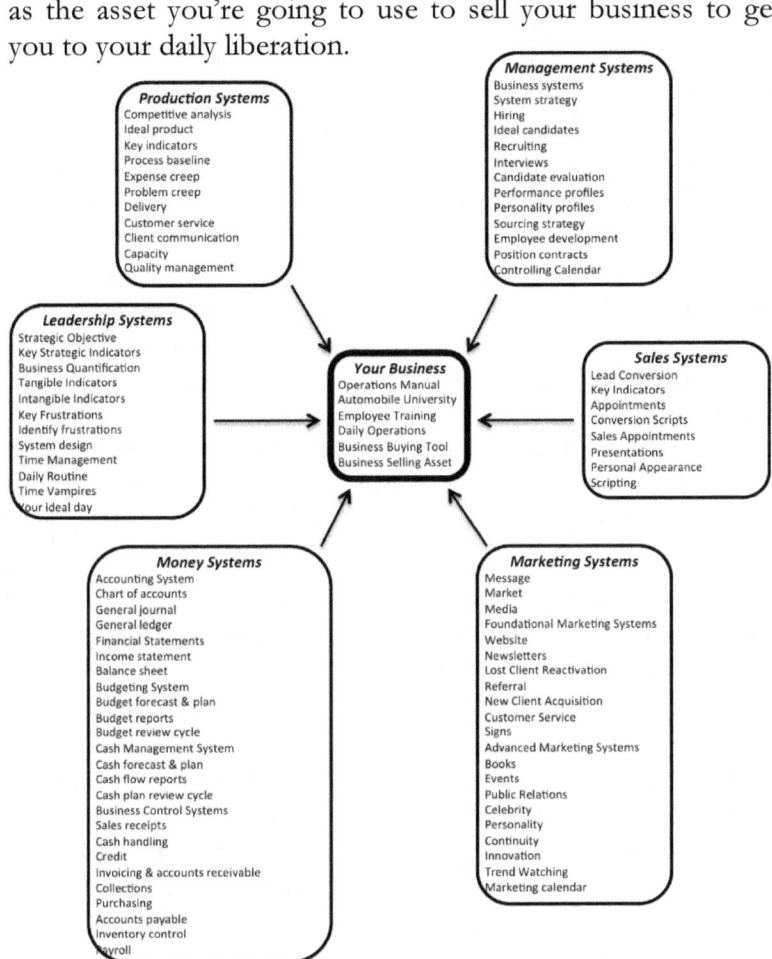

Production Systems
Competitive analysis
Ideal product
Key indicators
Process baseline
Expense creep
Problem creep
Delivery
Customer service
Client communication
Capacity
Quality management

Management Systems
Business systems
System strategy
Hiring
Ideal candidates
Recruiting
Interviews
Candidate evaluation
Performance profiles
Personality profiles
Sourcing strategy
Employee development
Position contracts
Controlling Calendar

Leadership Systems
Strategic Objective
Key Strategic Indicators
Business Quantification
Tangible Indicators
Intangible Indicators
Key Frustrations
Identify frustrations
System design
Time Management
Daily Routine
Time Vampires
Your ideal day

Your Business
Operations Manual
Automobile University
Employee Training
Daily Operations
Business Buying Tool
Business Selling Asset

Sales Systems
Lead Conversion
Key Indicators
Appointments
Conversion Scripts
Sales Appointments
Presentations
Personal Appearance
Scripting

Money Systems
Accounting System
Chart of accounts
General journal
General ledger
Financial Statements
Income statement
Balance sheet
Budgeting System
Budget forecast & plan
Budget reports
Budget review cycle
Cash Management System
Cash forecast & plan
Cash flow reports
Cash plan review cycle
Business Control Systems
Sales receipts
Cash handling
Credit
Invoicing & accounts receivable
Collections
Purchasing
Accounts payable
Inventory control
Payroll

Marketing Systems
Message
Market
Media
Foundational Marketing Systems
Website
Newsletters
Lost Client Reactivation
Referral
New Client Acquisition
Customer Service
Signs
Advanced Marketing Systems
Books
Events
Public Relations
Celebrity
Personality
Continuity
Innovation
Trend Watching
Marketing calendar

Figure 5.4

Leadership Systems

The first type of system that should be in place are the leadership systems. Now before I go into which systems at a minimum should be in place, let's define leadership and it's role in the business for the purposes of systems documentation. The key element to develop through leadership is vision, your vision of what the business looks like now and what it will look like in the future. Vision is your dream for the future, what the business will look like when it is fully developed, it is your strategic objective. It will keep in mind the long-term objectives of the company while managing the company on a day to day basis.

Most businesses are started by people who understand the technical work and operations of the business, but do not realize that this is really working IN the business. To be a true leader you must learn to work ON your business, become the entrepreneur that understands the technical operations but works on the operations of a technical business instead of being the owner who performs the technical operations and works 100% IN the business.

> To be a good leader in your business you must learn how to and find the time to work ON your business.

To work ON your business there are four areas you'll need to systematize at a minimum and these areas are your strategic objective, your key strategic indicators, your key frustrations and time management.

I have a client that works in the oilfield production industry and he was explaining to me that he's already got all of this done and then proceeded to walk me through his offices and pointed to pictures on the wall. One of them said 'teamwork' and had a great picture of people working hard and then he showed me the next one that said 'dedication' and another great high gloss photo of people dedicated to their work. He thought that's what great leadership was, just some fancy expensive pictures on the wall. But that's not what this type of leadership is about. This leadership is about you taking command of your business in a real, tactile manner and documenting what your vision for the future of the company is. You don't need to put this vision in a frame and hang it on the wall, but you do need to communicate it in a very real way to your staff, your employees so they understand that you really mean what you say and that your vision is where the company is going and not some fancy sign on the wall.

Your strategic objective is a clearly written picture of your company's future and is written in two stages. The first stage is to write a basic description of your business and stage two is to make it unique and distinguishable amongst your competitors. We spoke at length about this and the previous module when we discussed your company story in your unique selling proposition. This is in essence the constitution of your business, it is dynamic in nature changed only occasionally in response to major shifts in your competition and market trends. If you look at your worksheets you'll see on the first few pages we have a strategic objective worksheet. This talks about some of the basics such as what line of business and product you're in, what company size and what your growth objectives on a year-to-year basis. What is the geographic scope, where are your target markets what is your marketing position. We'll talk about a general description of your target market, the age of your market, the timing such as how long do you want to be in this business and when will these objectives be obtained. This discusses competition, what is your competitive advantage, price, quality, convenience and what are the distinctive elements of your product or service. It also talks about enhancements you can make to your product or service, now a lot of these things are parts of the system's documentation process. So you will tie all of this in to this leadership face. You also see quite a few of my own personal examples within the workbook.

Your key strategic indicators are the quantification of your business as they relate to your strategic objective. They focus on the critical elements of your systems to tell you how the business is progressing toward your strategic objective. These indicators measure both tangible and non-tangible operations of your business. The non-tangible ones tend to be the ones that many Westerners ignore such as how your employee's morale is, but there really is no number to put into that form until now, using this worksheet. There is a business classification worksheet in the workbook that allows you to take those non-tangible operations of your business and put them into a tangible indicator so that you can see where things are currently and where they were before especially as they relate to your strategic objective. So use these business qualification worksheets to help make your goals into a reality. These numbers give you an objective violation of your business and are extremely useful when taking a new business on such as when you purchase another company. This will allow you to determine the health of the new acquisition through the use of your key strategic indicators. This is also beneficial when you go to sell your company you will be able to show your potential buyers document a proof of exactly how your business is progressing. So there will be no guessing of these non-tenable business operations, you will be able to show them with tangible numbers.

The key frustration process is your method to think systemically. It is your tool to cope with frustrations and problems as well as to take advantage of opportunities in your business. Many entrepreneurs think of problems as something that needs to be gotten rid of. The strategic entrepreneur will think of these frustrations and problems as opportunities to expand the business and to take advantage of these problems financially. It allows you to reduce people problems and screen out inaccurate perceptions about your business and to eliminate frustrations by creating effective systems to cure any underlying problems. The key frustration processes outlined in detail in the worksheet section of how you're going to go ahead and identify those frustrations and take advantage of them through profitable opportunities for your business.

Managing your time is about maximizing your most precious, irreplaceable resource. Effective use of your time, more than any other habit, will increase your productivity and your effectiveness as a leader. It is important to understand how much of your time is spent on productive activities that directly contribute to your strategic objective and how much is spent unproductively and moves you further away from your strategic objective. There are worksheets in the workbook that allow you to identify what you spend your time on and help you to maximize the use of that time and turn those wasted opportunities into productive activities. So for example in my own business I found that having an open door policy was a terrible idea, a terrible time waster of mine. I was always combating employees would come in and interrupt my workflow. So for the use of these worksheets identified that was a time waster and by getting rid of my open-door policy increase my own personal productivity. The key here is to have a system to identify when your most precious resource, time, is being used ineffectively.

These systems lend themselves very well to the Information Systems documentation method I instructed you on in the previous section on Systems Documentation. Audio recordings and Automobile University will be some great end products produced to train your employees and communicate your message.

Brainstorming Checklist

- ➤ Strategic Objective
- ➤ Key Strategic Indicators
- ➤ Business Quantification worksheet
- ➤ Measurable/Tangible Indicators
- ➤ Non-Measurable/Intangible Indicators
- ➤ Key Frustrations
  - Identify frustrations

- System design and Implementation
- Time Management
  - Daily Routine/Time Log
  - Time Vampires-Where does you time go
  - Outline your ideal day and plan to have it

Management Systems

Management is all about getting things done, not about you doing things. It is not the same as leadership, it's not about vision, it is about how you get things done in your business without you having to do those things. In a nutshell management is about systematization of your business. It's about taking input of various sorts, engaging them and changing them through a process and producing a desired output. Systems free your people to pay attention to things that matter while the routine things take care of themselves while raising the performance of your people.

Your systems development was detailed in our previous module and here you can see in the worksheet the interrelation between all the business systems in your business

You start your management with your organizational structure, the military calls this a chain of command and all good businesses have a well thought out well-organized chain of command. Many experts have this graphical representation of a business's corporate structure as mostly horizontal with very little middle management. Regardless of how your business is organized it is still important to make sure that you have a graphical representation of your management structure. And create positions within that structure with the goal of being able to meet your strategic objective with the positions listed in this organizational structure. This begins with a graphic representation of your company's organizational structure with positions created to allow you to reach your strategic objective.

> Develop your own business systems strategy diagram so you can have a visual representation of the organization of your business.

Controlling calendar is also an appointment calendar and a daily prioritizer. It is an infinitely flexible tool that will provide a structure for advanced planning, give you an immediate at a glance view of work in progress and status. It reminds you of what you have to do for other people, what they have to do for you as well as helps you avoid conflict and capture the history of each project to show you what's working and what's not. There are many types of software available for contractors that can do this for you as long as in some way and in some format you have a calendar that will allow you to control your own day and prioritize your own work. Now there are worksheets in the blueprints manual that have controlling calendar documents, daily prioritizers, and other examples.

Recruiting process helps you bring the right people to your door and is really a form of marketing and lead generation activity to help you find the right employees instead of clients. So you're going to take the same skills that we mentioned in phase 1 with foundational and advanced marketing and apply those same and tactics and strategies to your recruiting process to find the right employees. Because marketing is all about finding the right people, we talked about finding the right clients but recruiting is about finding the right employees.

Hiring is choosing the right people for your team and is really the most consequential decision process for your business. You now have an objective system you can put into place to allow you to effectively interview and hire the right people to operate your systems and achieve your strategic objective. There is a system in the worksheets section that I have personally used for many years as well as it has received many accolades from business experts. It is called the top grading system. It is a way to screen all of your interviewees to make sure they are the right person for the position. While this is a slower process is very effective in finding a right person, remember, be slow to hire and quick to fire. Will find in these worksheets on top grading that this interview style focuses primarily on work history and education because the history of how the employee behaved in the past will tell you a lot about how the employee will behave in the future and the questions in this process bring this to light. The top grading format goes in much deeper than any resume possibly can and has saved me from the wrong hires on multiple occasions. On occasion even with this system I have made the wrong higher, but when I went back and reviewed the interview forms and notes we took I found some commonalities between all of the people that I hired that with the wrong fit for the job. On many occasions I would hire based solely on previous military experience, but I didn't look deeply enough as the top grading process dictates. What I found was when these prior military personnel were discharged under other than honorable conditions we would have problems as well. So I had to fire them at some point but I could've seen this had I looked in deeper into the interview process. Another revelation came in the copying process the when we realized that all of the bad hires were highly musically inclined, they frequently had to be fired very early in their employment. The reason was because although they were very technically talented they were frequently up late at night playing their music and therefore showed up often late to work and not well rested to perform at their peak capacity during work hours. So for us this was not a good fit.

Position contracts give your employees the road maps for their success with a written contract between management and employee with explicit standards and accountability for the work they produce. The position contract is in essence an action plan, such as we discussed in the previous section. This gives your employees a detailed contract of what you expect from them and you can see this throughout the examples in the worksheets I have provided for you.

Developing people and getting them to achieve beyond their current limitations is crucial to growing your business. People problems are the number one most common frustration facing entrepreneurs and businesses and solving these frustrations and developing your people can be accomplished with a proper and documented employee development system. In a recent Gallup poll the reason given by employees that leave a company 82% of the time is because of their manager, their direct supervisor. So investing time and energy in developing your people can save you many thousands of dollars in replacing employees alone. It's worth the time and effort to get this documented and implemented in your business just as we discussed in a previous section with automobile university. All of this gives your management team the tools to use to lead their own people and increase employee retention.

Brainstorming Checklist

➤ Business systems
  • Generic system strategy worksheet
➤ Hiring
  • Ideal candidates
  • Recruiting
    ✓ Leverage higher pay for longer term key positions
  • Interviews
    ✓ Topgrading
    ✓ Fascinate
  • Candidate evaluation
  • Performance profiles
  • Personality profiles
  • Sourcing strategy
➤ Employee development
➤ Position contracts
➤ Controlling Calendar

Money Systems

Accounting Systems – explains accounting from the viewpoint of the business owner rather than the accountant. It also provides guidelines for getting the most out of your accountant and your accounting system. You'll be able to understand and use accounting information to make better decisions. Many entrepreneurs know some of the key numbers in their business in but they still must have an well-developed accounting system in place so that all of these numbers can make sense and help to make better decisions in some way. And we will go through the details in the money worksheets in the blueprints manual so you can understand or at least take these systems, develop them to use to train your own staff. Use the worksheets as examples and templates to develop your own accounting system.

Financial Statements – explains the two most important financial statements, the Balance Sheet and the Income Statement. It shows you how to understand what they mean in terms of the financial health of your company, and how to use them to monitor your business' performance and detect problems and opportunities. As the CEO these statements are of utmost importance to you in the decision-making process. These statements are ones you will want to know in intimate detail and understand how they affect the day-to-day operations of your business. Not only will they play a key role in the operation of your company, but they will also play a key role when it comes time to acquire other companies. Also, when potential buyers of your company come to the bargaining table they will want to see these very same financial statements as well. In the blueprints minimal worksheets you will find instructions on how to do a detailed evaluation of all of the pertinent financial statements.

Budgeting Systems - provides you with the basic tool for the financial management of your company. Your operating budget enables you to plan every aspect of your business and to track your progress in comparison with the plan. Budget "variance analysis" is a simple technique for automatically highlighting strengths and weaknesses of your business. This serves as a key strategic indicator when it comes to determining the health of the business and help me to determine when we were spending too much money in certain areas as well as when we weren't spending enough money in other areas such as marketing. An example of this is when in my own industrial repair business I noticed month-to-month we were spending over the budgeted amount on parts costs. After some investigation it was discovered that we had switched vendors and the new vendor wasn't giving us the discounts the previous vendor had. There were also other times when I realized that we were spending under the budgeted amount for our marketing efforts, it came to my attention that we weren't printing our newsletters in color because of a cost-saving activity. So monitoring the budgeting systems help me to see different activities going on in the business because I knew how to use this system to help me run the company. In the money worksheets and a blueprint's mantle you'll again find much more detail about the budgeting systems. There are many very methodical questions that you can use to determine key strategic indicator performance in your business.

Cash Management Systems - gives you control over the lifeblood of your business - cash. It shows you how to track and control the cash moving into, out of, and within your business. It also shows you where there may be hidden cash within your business, and how to get the most out of your cash resources.

Business Control Systems - describes how to use your normal business activities to generate the financial information you need to run your company, how that information feeds into your accounting system, and how the business control systems can generate reports that will tell you immediately and in detail exactly what's going right and what's going wrong so you can do something about it. The blueprints manual worksheets also includes a business control systems report card to show you all the detailed areas within your business systems that you want to have well-documented procedures for.

Brainstorming Checklist

- ➤ Accounting System
    - Chart of accounts
    - General journal
    - General ledger
- ➤ Financial Statements
    - Income statement Balance sheet
- ➤ Budgeting System
    - Budget forecast & plan
    - Budget reports
    - Budget review cycle
- ➤ Cash Management System
    - Cash forecast & plan
    - Cash flow reports
    - Cash plan review cycle
- ➤ Business Control Systems
    - Sales receipts
    - Cash handling
    - Credit
    - Invoicing & accounts receivable
    - Collections
    - Purchasing
    - Accounts payable
    - Inventory control
        - ✓ Raw materials inventory
        - ✓ Work in progress inventory

- ✓ Finished goods inventory
- ✓ Scrap inventory
- ➤ Payroll

Marketing Systems

Marketing systems are the foundational and advanced pieces of a direct response system to keep selling to your current clients and generate referrals. These are also the systems to reactivate lost clients as well as generate new leads and turn them into clients as well. With a profitable direct marketing system in place this positions you optimally to purchase other companies as well as make your business worth more and become more desirable to potential buyers.

Message, your unique selling proposition and your story are what sets you apart from everyone else and you can accomplish this by answering the following question: Why would my client do business with me versus any other option available to them, including doing nothing at all?

Market is knowing in detail who your ideal client is and where they are most likely to be found. Demographics and psychographics play a large role in knowing who your clients are and creating a visual representation of them in an avatar helps you to visualize them even better. Demographics for residential HVAC and Plumbing customers are usually MUCH less important than where they are located and your market share (which varies zip code-by-zip code) compared to your hundreds of competitors. Very few homeowners will buy new heating or cooling systems unless the one they own now is broken, expensive to operate or not adequately heating/cooling their home.

It doesn't matter what your advertising agency, radio rep or other advisors say about the Life Style attributes of their audience. You sell or service plumbing or HVAC systems that aren't working properly. For financial reasons, your customers are most often "old people with money". After looking at twenty-five million customer records we've found that very few good customers are under the age of 40 and most are much older than that, because that's where the wealth is.

Media – Often and incorrectly the first thing many businesses focus on. The media should be used to cater to the right market with the right media.

Foundational Marketing Systems

Website must be a direct response based website format to capture new leads and follow up with existing leads and turn them into clients and/or have them feed your sales funnel.

Newsletters are the backbone to maintaining a fence around your herd for your light commercial clients. It will take form in printed as well as online formats to achieve maximum exposure as well as it will have a customized message enabling you to reach each major category of client you have.

Lost Client Reactivation - An often overlooked category of clients though actually the third best type of client to reintroduce to your products. They already know your services so we will reintroduce them to you and let them know they have not been forgotten as well as address any past issues.

Referral - Your referral program will gain you new business from your second best client type, referrals from existing clients. You will have a program that takes advantage of the strong relationship you have with your existing clients.

New Client - Acquisition Many times businesses leap to gaining new clients only to realize that they are the most expensive type of client to get. We will initiate a complete sales funnel to reach your ideal clients types and help you grow the business with them.

Customer Service - How your company handles clients is critical to client retention. Now there are many ways that customer service ties into marketing. Such as in person greetings and transactions, phone transactions and email transactions.

Signs- Perception is reality and if you have signs of any type then this program will remove the platitudes on your signs and replace them with direct marketing based signage.

Advanced Marketing Systems

Events - Getting your clients into a place where you can sell to them in a one to many environment is so effective that entire industries exist just to do this. You will have a new way to introduce new and existing products and services to all of your client types (existing, referral, lost and new) and achieve higher sales in a condensed time period. Events can take the shape of small 2 or 3 person group tours of your facility or office to great events with thousands of people in an exhibit hall, all there to see you. No matter what the event looks like it can be a tremendously valuable way for you to build stronger client relationships and boost your business sales. Home Shows are a perfect example of an Event in a foundational market system.

Public Relations - Free publicity in any area of the country is very powerful. Whether your clients are local or national or both, publicity through news media, television, radio or magazines adds tremendous credibility and builds trust with your clients. There are many advantages to publicity, it can be cheap, it provides instant credibility, very fast to get to the market, it can be really fun and boosts you to a celebrity status within your market. More and more contractors are using charity sponsorships like wrapping a truck pink for the Koman Race for the Cure to garner free publicity.

Celebrity - Building celebrity into your marketing also adds credibility and exposure for you. To find them first you must begin to think locally about current and previous celebrities. These people are not necessarily involved in your industry, it just must be someone that your clients would think highly of and have respect for. I know many businesses that have a male clientele that loves football. So, in the fall every year they hire a retired NFL player, not a great player, but a well know player that live locally and he comes out and sign autographs for the clients. This generate publicity as well as an event and adds credibility to the business.

Personality - Most businesses are quite boring to their clients, yes you probably very boring to your clients if all you talk about is your industry and how good you are at it. The problem with being boring is that you are trying to form a tighter relationship with your client and that requires you to let your client into your personal life a little. People buy from people and the stronger your relationship with your clients means that they will buy more and more often from you.

Continuity – Service Agreement programs where your clients pay you an ongoing fee whether they use your services or not. Sometimes referred to as residual income but with a little creativity continuity income and programs can be added to any type of business. I never thought it would work for my industry of electronic repairs but if you look at the examples I provided you will see that I was able to put continuity into industrial electronic repairs. Not an industry accustomed to month recurring charges I must tell you.

Innovation - New products and services – to existing clients. Selling IAQ, tank-less water heaters, water filtration, Duct Sealing etc. are proven ways to increase sales to existing customers on service calls.

Trend Watching - This is how you avoid being a victim of your own success, get rid of the blinders and become aware of your surroundings. Don't become the next Blockbuster Video or Circuit City or Betamax if you're old enough to remember that. Right now you see companies like Radio Shack desperately trying to reinvent themselves but it could have been avoided if they had made themselves aware of what's going on around them.

Brainstorming Checklist

- Message
- Market
- Media
- Foundational Marketing Systems
  - Website
  - Newsletters
  - Lost Client Reactivation
  - Referral
  - New Client Acquisition
  - Customer Service
  - Signs
- Advanced Marketing Systems
  - Books
  - Events
  - Public Relations
  - Celebrity
  - Personality
  - Continuity
- Innovation
- Trend Watching
- Marketing calendar

Sales Systems

Sales systems are how you give your clients the opportunity to say yes. They define your current lead generation systems, how to understand the key features of an effective lead conversion sales process and how to innovate to achieve effective systems for sales. I must say, very few industries devote more time and money week in and week out on sales training than residential HVAC or plumbing. But, LOTS of that training is going through the motions laid out in one of the many sales training manuals available to the industry. Its better than NOT training but not as effective as training aimed at realistic, achievable, high goals. Financially, the most important sales goal is your average new customer value. For successful contractors, that's where almost 70% of their sales comes from every year. If you want to have a business that is more valuable than your run of the mill contractor, then you need to focus on this number in your business.

Sales appointments systems orchestrate the interaction between your sales staff and your clients. Your lead conversion interactions depend on having presentations that address their purchase decision needs in the right way at the right time using scripting.

Your indicators for your sales conversion process are very important to make sure that you have documented as well. So within the worksheets of the blueprints manual you will find that there are baseline, previous and current periods of lead conversion and key strategic indicators that you can use in your own sales process. So use these worksheets as the tool to give yourself a jump-start on documenting your sales process.

Brainstorming Checklist

➢ Lead Conversion
  • Key indicators

- Appointments
- Conversion scripts
- Sales appointments
  - Presentations
  - Personal appearance
  - Scripting

Production Systems

Production systems are all about fulfilling the promises you made to your client. It's doing what you said you were going to do. Consistently. Predictably. Time after time. This system describes the key components of production including work flow, quality (fewer callbacks) and cost control and helps you improve your production process by evaluating, analyzing and innovating the individual systems that make up production in your business. Many entrepreneurs understand this part of process and it tends to be the most well documented portion of any system. What is often missing though is innovation in this process because entrepreneurs tend to fall in love with their own product or service. They tend to miss trend watching as part of the production system and making their products and services better suited as a solution for their client's problems.

Your delivery process helps you get your products in the hands of your clients in the most effective way by focusing on key points of channel selection, scheduling, reliability and cost control and the impact the delivery process has on your customers. Many times and an often overlooked part of the production process is the delivery of the product or service to the client. But this process is actually as important or even more important in some cases than a product or service itself, because the presentation of your product or service affects the value the client assigns to it. For example, if the product is delivered late or in a broken container or the product itself is damaged in some way this has a tremendous negative perception on the product as well as on your company. So making sure that your delivery process gives your product its best chance, it's best opportunity to show up in the best light increases the perceptive value of the product. In contrast of his delivered before expected, in a branded well handled package and everything looks to be in perfect shape there is a higher perceived value of the product. As well as if the product does not work as expected your clients will be much more lenient on you if everything else in the delivery process worked flawlessly.

Your customer service process clarifies the nature of customer services in your business and helps you innovate your client service process to improve both the perception and the reality of your business and your products in the eyes of your clients. The worksheets contain a tremendous amount of valuable information for you to use to document your production systems. Just as in the delivery process the customer service process plays a key role in the perception of your product or service. If there is a consistency with which how the client is handled each time and every time than the perception is that the products and services will perform consistently and will therefore have a higher perceived value. Every time you improve interactions with your clients, any touch points with your product or service, you increase the perceived value.

Brainstorming Checklist

- ➤ Production Systems
  - • Competitive analysis
  - • Ideal product
  - • Key indicators
    - ✓ Process baseline
    - ✓ Expense creep
    - ✓ Problem creep
- ➤ Delivery
- ➤ Customer service
- ➤ Client communication
- ➤ Capacity
- ➤ Quality management

Chapter 6

Growth On Steroids

Why Use Acquisitions For Growth?

Acquiring other businesses can be the most viable and exciting method to grow your business rapidly and more profitably than just growing it organically through marketing and sales growth alone. It is the 'secret sauce' for Cisco, Microsoft, Google, Starbucks and now Facebook for bulking up and becoming mega corporations in less than ten years from their founding. This is the power of the system that is being unveiled to you in this chapter, so you will need to pay close attention.

Acquisitions involve taking control of other businesses that could literally double or triple your company revenue, client base, number of employees and geographic footprint overnight. It is a standard and frequently used growth strategy for larger corporations, but is a seldom used and infrequently modeled strategy for the large majority of entrepreneurs because they lack the knowledge or skills for executing it as a growth weapon. You really can't blame yourself for this because acquisitions are made to look really hard to accomplish by industry jargon and big words that seem really complex. Organic growth is like driving a car to get you from point a to point b. Acquisitions is like taking a fighter jet to get you there. Sure the fighter jet takes more skill and practice but once you use it, you'll fly it everywhere!

Are you ready to take the next logical step? Schedule your contractor market assessment. So you can identify the prospects that are 600 X more likely to turn into a new customer...and it's FREE too!
Simply go to www. MEERScore.com/freeoffer and fill out the application for a 45 minute phone call with Mike Layton.

As a special bonus, this includes an additional FREE strategy session to get your customized plan for exponential growth with Walter Bergeron.

The Slow Model

There are any-number of ways to grow your business through acquisitions. One of the most commonly thought of ways amongst blue-collar entrepreneurs is to buy another business just like the one you already have. A commercial cleaner buys another commercial cleaning business or an exterminator buys another pest control services company. This is the simplest and most common way growth is thought about when it comes to the acquisitions growth model. You are in essence buying out your competitors to expand capabilities, possibly expand geographic territories and maybe even to reach a "critical mass" which may get your brand recognized more often and "out there". Earlier, we pointed out that your cost effective organic growth will probably come in 8-10 zip codes.

> There is another more focused method to take maximum advantage of the risks inherent in any type of acquisition. If you are going to take the risk, make the reward as big as possible.

In the 30-90 zip codes where organic growth is difficult for the typical contractor growing my acquiring a competitor who is stronger than you in 10 of these zip codes is a proven strategy whether you are the buyer or the seller. What you should know though, is that there is another much more focused way to take maximum advantage of the risks inherent in any type of acquisition. A method that has the same possibilities of failure and success but that leverages all this risk with the potential for much, much greater reward. That process of exponential growth is what I call the growth-stacking model.

The Growth-Stacking Model

Growth stacking is the process of combining multiple methods of business growth simultaneously. More and more contractors are using this model with success. Plumbers are buying HVAC contractors, HVAC contractors are buying Home Security Systems companies, Electricians are buying

Solar Companies, etc. Instead of giving you the nitty-gritty details to start off with, let me tell you about one of my clients, Gerald.

Gerald owns a pest control company, he's an exterminator by trade, meaning he goes into peoples' houses and gets rid of their bugs and unwanted pests. He is a humble, but driven, blue-collar entrepreneur and I consider it my calling to guide him to his financial liberation. So Gerald's pest control company was grossing around $600k in annual revenue and around 10% profit. A comfortable living for him and his wife and children but nowhere near large enough to reach his retirement goal, he calls it his enough is enough number.

The process of exponential growth through growth stacking works like this. Basically, Gerald would seek out and strategically buy other companies and merge them with his company. Then he would use 3 growth models and exponentially grow his company and then sell the much larger, much more profitable company after he reached his growth goal and someone offered him his enough is enough number for the business. For Gerald, that process looked like this:

He searched for a company that:

1. Had around the same gross revenue as his company, so he could afford to do this deal comfortably.

Actually, the way this deal was structured Gerald walked away from the closing with many thousands of dollars in his pocket, through a process called a full leveraged buyout.

2. Had the same type of clients but no overlap between his current clients and the acquisition company clients

3. He made sure there was lots of duplication of company business processes.

And I'll get into why he wanted that in a second.

Once he found a company that met these three goals he made the purchase.

Gerald executed step one and made a...

Strategic Acquisition

At closing his *$600k business became a $1.2 million company*, not a bad day to be able to double the size of your company at the stroke of a pen.

But this is just the tip of the iceberg when it comes to Growth-Stacking.

Step two of Growth-Stacking is called the...

Cross Marketing Multiplier

Do you remember when I told you that Gerald bought a company that met his goals? You might have noticed that none of his goals for his Strategic Acquisition of the right company had anything to do with the type of services they offered, just that they had identical client types.

Gerald actually bought an air conditioning company, an HVAC company, just like yours. Now Gerald certainly could have bought another pest control company, to most entrepreneurs this would be the most logical choice, stick with what you know.

But Gerald was thinking strategically and used Growth Stacking to maximize the amount of his growth.

He knew that by acquiring another company and focusing on the client that the services weren't a critical criteria for the purchase. As a matter of a fact, had Gerald

---

bought another pest control company *he would not have been able to take advantage of the Cross Marketing Multiplier.*

The Cross Marketing Multiplier works like this.
Gerald took his pest control services and offered those services to his newly acquired clients and in a very short time, since he already had a great relationship with his clients from the purchase of the new business, he quickly increased his revenue by another multiple. Gerald marketed his pest control service to the air conditioning clients, **using the marketing system we put into place in preparation for this acquisition** and went from $1.2 million to $1.8 million. **But Gerald certainly didn't stop there.** He then took his newly acquired air conditioning services and offered those services to his pest control clients. And since he had a great relationship with those clients as well *Gerald's company went from $1.8 million to $2.4 million.* This is something impossible to do without a Strategic Acquisition. (see Figure 6.1) **There is no faster or easier way to double the size of your client list** AND have that very critical already established bond, that well developed relationship with your clients, all with the stroke of a pen. And it is because of this previously established relationship that the Cross Marketing Multiplier works. But Gerald didn't stop there either. Remember that one of Gerald 's criteria for the company he was going to buy was that they had a duplication of business processes, meaning that both companies had a human resources department and accounting and sales and marketing departments and personnel and equipment. Well, as a savvy entrepreneur, Gerald implemented step three of growth-stacking called...

Efficiency Profits
Efficiency profits increases growth by another multiple by eliminating all of the duplication between the two companies. By eliminating duplicate expenses in personnel, real estate, business equipment, this change increases profits

substantially. Then on top of the elimination of expenses you add back in efficiency by keeping the best of the best parts of both business processes. These two factors enabled Gerald to add another multiple of value to the company while at the same time increasing profits by another 10%.

Part one, Gerald did one *Strategic Acquisition* and on day one at the closing he doubled the size of his company from *$600k to $1.2* million and walked out of the deal with no up front costs and with a few thousand dollars in his pocket by doing a fully leveraged buyout.

Part two, Gerald implemented the *Cross Marketing Multiplier* and within a few months he had cross-marketed the services of both companies, since he now had a list of clients that doubled in size at the closing.

So he went from *$1.2 million to $1.8* million by selling air conditioning services to pest control clients and then went from *$1.8 million to $2.4* million by offering his pest control services to his air conditioning clients.

Then part three he implemented *Efficiency Profits* and eliminated duplicate expenses and increased the efficiency of both companies and went from *$2.4 million to $3 million dollars*. So with Growth Stacking his business size increased by 5 times and his profits went from 10% of $600k, so $60k to 20% of $3 million, that's $600k.

That's an increase in profits of 10 times! (see Figure 6.1)
And he did all of this in less than 12 months from closing.
That's the power of a properly executed, well-engineered strategic acquisition.

And now since Gerald was more experienced in the Growth Stacking process he did this once more and this time shot the size of his business up to over *$12 million only 24 months later.*

No Promises Here

Now I want to emphasize that **I cannot promise or guarantee that you can do this**, you need to make this decision and decide if this is right for you. But, I would urge you to do a little homework and look at how large companies are making huge moves through acquisitions. Look at what venture capitalists are doing, and look at what the large players in your market are doing to achieve massive growth and market share. I think you will find that strategic acquisitions play a large role and that it would be a great opportunity for you to exponentially grow your business.

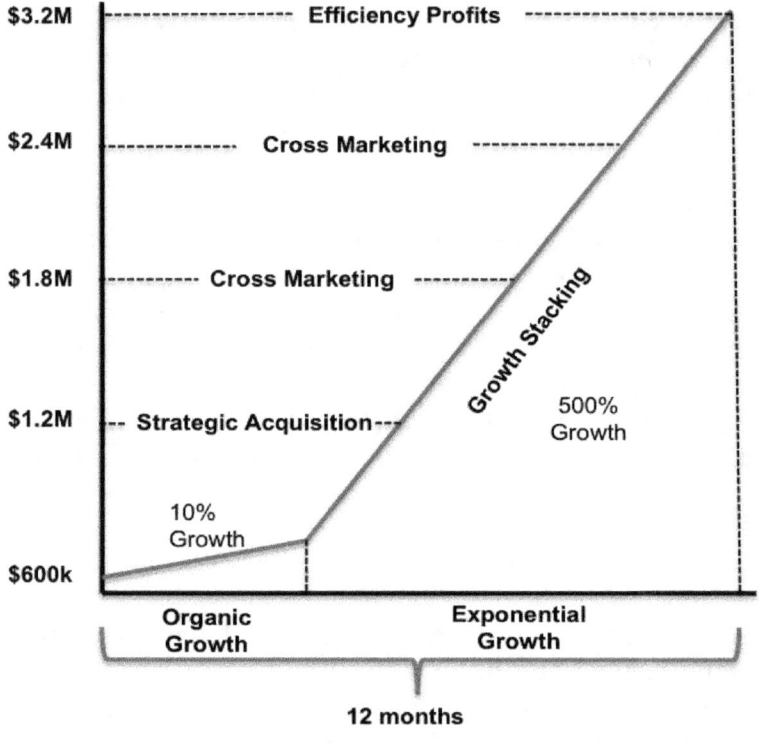

Figure 6.1

Starting With The end In Mind

The growth-stacking model strategy is really about starting with the end in mind. The goal is to get to the eight-figure level as quickly as possible and the real difference between this model and the slow organic growth model is time. With limitless time the slow growth model works, but it may take decades to reach the same level of growth that growth-stacking can achieve in as little as 2 years. Time is also a critical factor when it comes to selling the business. One of the criteria that comes into play for the eventual sales price of your business will be the rate of growth. You will get a higher price for your business if you have grown from $600k to $10 million in only 2 years than you would if you did the same amount of growth in 10 years. Slow growth is not the same as quick, exponential growth. A buyer, any buyer, will see your business as tremendously more valuable if your year to year growth is in the 500% range, rather than the 10, 20 or 30% range. There is no comparison! Money is attracted to speed! Growth stacking gets you to 8 figures faster and will get you a larger payday when it comes time to sell, period, end of story!

Complimentary versus Same-Same

If you were to use the old strategy of buying another company exactly like yours, you will have a very limited pool of sellers to select from. In order to get an exponentially larger pool to choose from you must first select an industry of companies with products or services that compliment the services you currently offer. So the exterminator won't just have to look to purchase one of the 20 other pest control companies in his geographic area. He will be able to select his acquisition target from the 20 kitchen remodelers, plus the 20 HVAC companies, plus the 20 residential cleaners, plus the 20 home automobile detailers, etc.... This makes the problem of finding the perfect target infinitely easier when you have such a huge selection pool to start with.

Finding A Complimentary Business

So how do you go about finding a business or industry that will fit and be complimentary to your existing business? Do you just close your eyes and throw a dart at a page in the phone book? One of the most common myths is that you have to guess at what kind of business would be best for you to purchase and hope and pray that it works out. Hope the business meshes well with your existing company and pray you pick a product or service that your clients will like. Well, not exactly. Actually you start with your clients first. They always come first. Any other way of selecting a complimentary product or services is a terrible plan and should be avoided at all costs. There is a much better way to do this and substantially increase the chances of success. Ask!

It probably sounds foolishly easy, but it is so often an overlooked option. Business owners tend to think that they know what their clients want. I know I did and sometimes still do. That's an error that should be avoided at all costs. Though, it's how many of us got our start in our business isn't it? We went out and bought all the equipment, learned the skills, leased or bought a building and then and only then did we go out and hope we could get enough customers to buy from us that we could support our self and the business. Well, now it's time to move to a much more sophisticated model with a higher likelihood of success, we ask.

Ask And Test

The "ask and test" process starts with being observant while you are with your clients. See what they are doing, observe what other products and services they are using and buying. There is no need to guess, you'll see what's going on. When you pull up to their home or their office, notice if there is a truck delivering a product or performing another service. I had a client that noticed one of his clients routinely had a coffee supply truck delivering coffee supplies a couple of times a month. So this prompted the next step, ask. Asking about what other services or products can be as easy as making a list of your observations and then having a casual conversation with your client. Or you can get a little more sophisticated and leave behind a quick five question survey for your client to fill out at his leisure. A couple of particular clients come to mind that this survey method worked very well for. Gerald, whom I mentioned earlier, owns a pest control company and leaves surveys behind with a self-addressed and stamped envelope. The survey has a few questions at a time about the services he observed his clients were using and he gathered some immensely valuable information from this technique. The exact same method also worked for a commercial cleaning entrepreneur, he leaves behind a survey and waits for the responses to arrive by mail a few days later. Effective, yet easy.

Armed with answers from the surveys, now it's time to test out the information gathered. Gerald, my pest control client, first tested coffee services. He found a competing coffee service company and formed a quick strategic partnership with them. He would earn a commission when he sold their services to his clients. This is an advanced technique to be able to actually get paid to test what your clients want, not to mention very effective. For about three months Gerald used his marketing skills, which went over in previously, to sell a number of coffee service contracts. After a few more months Gerald examined the possibility of purchasing a coffee service company. He eventually decided that this wouldn't work out due to the lower margins and number of clients he would have to have to make a good return on investment. This service just didn't match his client list size, he would have to have sold 100% of his clients the coffee service just to break even. This test didn't work out, but he did use the testing process to test a number of other services and found out that an HVAC service met all of this needs perfectly. So, after testing the market by servicing and selling air conditioners he eventually purchased an HVAC company. Then he did it over and over again to find another target for acquisition. Ask, test, and then repeat.

Finding Motivated Sellers

After completing multiple ask and test trials, you will have yourself a list of at least five types of businesses that would be a great, complimentary fit for your company. But now what? How do you find motivated sellers? You will have already exponentially increased the size of your list many times over the old way of finding potential sellers because you are looking at multiple business types rather than just one, but now let's expand the pool again by not just looking at businesses up for sale, let's look at all possible targets.

When a business is put up for sale, it takes substantial time and effort to get it listed and onto the market for potential buyers to see. The problem is that most businesses don't sell! That's right, more often than not a business that is put up for sale the first time does not sell, so the seller takes it off the market after a certain period of time. Discouraged by the inability to sell it at the asking price, the seller often just gets back to work in the business. The fact that the business is not on the market does not mean that they don't want to sell it though. There are also business owners that either want to sell and just have not yet put their business up for sale or there are business owners that get overwhelmed by all the work it takes to prepare a business for sale, so they don't list it at all. No matter what the reason, we are going to take advantage of these situations and exponentially increase the size of our pool of sellers by making sure we look at these businesses as potential targets too.

Since we will be looking for businesses for sale both on the market and off the market, we will need to expand where we look. Typically, a buyer will go to online business listings as well as hire a business broker to find businesses for sale. We'll do that too, but we'll take it a lot further than these two simplistic approaches. We are going to put together a list of criteria of what we are looking for in a potential target acquisition and we are going to use every source of contact we can to find these targets. Here is a list of the minimum sources for potential targets to use:

1. Vendors

Your number one source for information on businesses for sale is your current list of vendors. They have to know what's going on in their industry, they know who's making money and who is not. They know who has good credit and who does not. They know which businesses are for sale and for how much. If you want to know the truth about businesses in your city, cultivate your relationship with your vendors.

2. Business For Sale Websites

This is the low hanging fruit, but the issue is that everyone knows this source and everyone goes there. Here are some of them: www.bizbuysell.com, www.mergerplace.com, www.mergernetwork.com and other similar online market place.

3. Cold Canvas and Search – via the Internet

Every salesperson knows this one. You can search the internet for business information and then knock on doors or call on the telephone to reach out to the business owner. All these ways work well, but you have to get past the feeling that you're intruding, you're not. Business owners and managers generally are pleased to talk about their business.

4. Promotion

Let the world know that you are looking for businesses to buy. Pass the word to everyone you know and meet and let them be voluntary bird dogs for you. The late W. Clement Stone got his first insurance business acquisition this way, and that became the platform for his multibillion-dollar insurance business.

5. Lawyers

Establish a friendly relationship with yours and others too. They're involved in probate sales and the settling of estates so, of course, they know about businesses for sale. You'll eventually need a lawyer when you close your business purchases, so get to know a good one who specializes in business.

6. CPAs/Accountants
Guess who has the books on businesses in your community? And often the CPAs and accountants are involved in the sale of their client's business. In any case, they have the inside knowledge you need, they know who's making money and how much, and who has a great, profitable operation. Use your contacts and establish a personal relationship with them.

7. Bookkeeping Services
This is the same as with Lawyers and CPA's but they also have another great reason for helping you out, you might become their client.

8. Stock Brokers
Often overlooked by business buyers, stock brokers can be an excellent source because they're sometimes involved in the sale of the stock of business corporations. Get to know a few of them and let them spread the word through their brokerage community. Like lawyers, CPAs and others, stock brokers are professionals and can be motivated by the promise of a finder's fee.

9. Bankers
Who should know more about the finances of local businesses than the banker? Sellers usually let their banker know they're selling, especially if outstanding business loans are involved. If you're not yet on a first-name basis with a banker, the time is now.

10. Wall Street Journal
Another of the better sources of information on businesses for sale. Look in the Businesses For Sale section. Watch out for the ads that list only a telephone number; when you call, they'll do their utmost to qualify you on the phone. Ads that

carry a P.O. Box number are best. The Journal is also a great newspaper in which to list your ads about your wants and needs.

11. Trade Journals

Every industry has dozens, even hundreds, of such publications devoted solely to it. There are trade journals for food service, hotels and motels, electronics, broadcasting, shipping, entertainment, automotive and on and on. Your vendor friends will usually have a few laying about their offices.

13. Real Estate Brokers

One of the better groups of professionals to be in touch with. Although normally concerned with real estate, the very nature of their industry brings them in touch with businesses for sale. They too like a finder's fee for helping you find businesses.

14. Telephone Book

A natural beginning for your cold canvassing. And you'll appreciate the Yellow Page system of listing businesses by category. The display ads will often give you a feel for the size and personality of the business.

15. Directories

Business and government organizations publish an almost endless array of them, listing businesses by type, size, location, etc. Look in the reference section of the public library. One of the best of sources for businesses to contact by telephone, letter or in person.

16. D & B

Dun and Bradstreet provides credit information and special reports on businesses. D & B charges for its services, but you may have a friendly contact who subscribes.

17. Chamber of Commerce

Your local Chamber provides essential information about the economic climate of the area. The Chamber will give you specific facts and figures about business trends and opportunities and acquaint you with ownership movement in local industries and businesses. In order to get a realistic feel of the business community, the Chamber is a must. It's also a great source of well-prepared material to include in your presentation to investors.

18. Better Business Bureau

Because the B.B.B. is the watchdog of business activities, you can quickly determine how a particular business is being received by the buying public; whether any complaints have been registered and how they have been resolved. The B.B.B. is a great agency to connect yourself with in your search for businesses to buy. If you can get acquainted with the staff, they'll often informally share information about businesses in transition that they're aware of.

19. Business Brokers

This source can be great or grim, depending on how you use the brokers and what you expect. If you want to contract for a broker to represent you, the buyer, that's one way. Usually, the broker you approach represents the seller, collects his/her fee from the seller and is legally obligated to get the best price and terms for the seller. Because of that arrangement, you should be ready to suffer the broker doing his/her best to qualify you before revealing much pertinent information.

20. Merger/Acquisition Companies

Much like business brokers only bigger and they deal in larger companies. Highly professional and a delight to work with.

21. Management Consultants

These individuals and firms are on the inside track of business and they often know what's going on before the news ever hits the streets. They also have priceless information about the current and potential worth of a business. Since they are professionals, you should assume that they deserve a fee for their effort in your behalf.

What To Look For

You will need to have established a detailed list of priorities and criteria for your acquisition targets to take this list to your source of leads. This list is also crucial to help to make sure that after the acquisition phase is complete that you are successful in running both companies. The priorities and criteria list is the place to start to make sure this exponential growth becomes a tremendous success.

Managing Growth

Managing growth potential is the primary reason to select acquisitions of companies that are complimentary and not identical to your original company. When it comes time to establishing the priorities and criteria you look for when selecting a target company for acquisition, it really comes down to being able to manage what you buy. You, of course, want to maximize the growth during the deal, but if you bite off more than you can chew and fail to manage the acquisition properly, then you are destined for utter failure. You certainly don't want to fail at such a large undertaking so set your priorities and criteria small at first and then build you skills for larger and more complex acquisitions later.

Size

An acquisition can be a daunting task to undertake especially when you add into the equation that you may as much as double the number of people you will be dealing with, both employees and clients. When it comes to your first acquisition the rule of thumb would be to start small. This is a marathon, not a sprint, so the experience and knowledge you gain from each subsequent deal will build you r skills tremendously. So, an advisable criteria for employee and revenue of your first acquisition would be no more than you currently have now. You can always go for bigger and larger companies during subsequent deals but let's focus on building your skills at first, then you can focus on shooting bigger fish in the barrel on later deals.

Another size criteria that plays a large role will be the size of the targets client list. First and foremost you must make sure they have a list of captured and documented clients with full contact details. Secondly they must have a quality list. If they haven't made contact with a client for months and months, should this really be considered as a client? This client list is all about the strength of the relationship they have. Again, in list size criteria, aim for a list with the same size and quality as yours is currently. If your list of existing clients is 1,000 and you stay in routine contact with that list at least monthly, then that is the same criteria you will use to judge the size and quality of the list of your target. Also, remember from the marketing chapter that there are multiple categories that your client list will fall into. The four types of clients are existing clients, referral clients, lost clients and new clients so ask about all four types when inquiring about the list with your target.

Geographic location

It's typically easier to manage another company when it's in close proximity to you. I almost made this critical mistake when I expanded into another state with a location that was 600 miles away. I had just taken over a location of another repair depot and I had to get it up and running with our systems and ways of doing things. Not to mention that I had to hire a staff for the location, train the staff and the myriad of tasks that are involved when getting this going. This came very close to failing simply because of the sheer number of hours it took to travel and the tremendous effort of 9 hours of traveling each way and doing this multiple times a month. It took a herculean effort to get things up and running smoothly and if I had to do this all over again and the option was available, I would have certainly selected a location closer to my headquarters. Make sure you take the location into consideration and at first I would recommend over estimating the time and effort it is going to take to do a lot of traveling to merge with a new acquisition.

Strengths and Weaknesses

Managing what you buy becomes much easier as your experience level with acquisitions improves, but it also is of great benefit if you select a target that has problems that you can solve easily. Your strengths are their weaknesses and their strengths are your weaknesses. All products and services have inherent weaknesses such as cost, delivery, people, timing, complicated processes, etc. This matchup makes the management of the transition have much higher odds for success because you already have the answer to upcoming problems and you won't need to go out and search for any solution that you don't already have. Knowing ahead of time that the matchup of strengths and weaknesses is already done makes the job of merging the acquisition much easier and just as important, faster.

For instance, your product or service may have weaknesses like seasonality. Air conditioning companies like my client Wade, had this issue and used an acquisition of a kitchen remodeling company to solve this weakness. Another problem you can solve in your business may be talent related or people. Your current company may for instance have a weak outside sales force. So, when selecting a company to acquire, one of your criteria may need to be that the target must have a strong outside sales force. This merger will make both companies stronger and this solution can be much faster than if you were to have to start your own outside sales force from scratch. This problem/solution process goes the other way too. If the target company has a poor performing business process such as accounting and you have done a great job in developing and documenting your accounting process, then the merger of the companies can quickly solve this problem. An added benefit to finding a target company with a serious problem is that you can use it to leverage down the price you pay and then once the acquisition is completed you can take that weakness, solve it quickly and have had the advantage of the poor performance play to your advantage in a significant way.

Ability to Pay for What You Intend to Buy

You must be able to pay for what you intend to buy. The price, the payment terms, and the subsequent cash flow of an acquisition will have an enormous impact on how your company might finance its purchase. You will, however, need to ensure that there are resources sufficient to not only close the transaction, but also to provide necessary working capital and other contributions to the acquired company's operations and future growth.

In determining how much you can afford pay to pay, and therefore an appropriate target size, you should carefully assess your company's financial strength and your appetite for risk. Add to these factors, a thorough evaluation of the historical financial results of the target company. Then use these considerations to develop pro forma statements that show the company's past results, with adjustments made as if it had been owned by your company as a corporate parent. Based on these analyses, you can develop projections factoring in the acquisition financing and terms.

The fact is that this part of the deal needs to involve your financial team such as your CPA and your lawyer, so get help to make sure you can afford the deal. Smartly acquired companies will largely pay for themselves from the target company's own earnings. Properly structured, this can often be done while still meeting the price requirements of the seller.

Team Building

To the uninitiated, acquisitions appear to be not for the meek at heart and you must be willing to step outside your comfort zone considerably. Acquisitions require the business owner to rally support from outside to bring in the resources required, mostly attracting expertise (not as employees but as independent advisors) in the various dimensions of the deal process as needed. Therefore, teambuilding is the major groundwork that you will need to have in place for your acquisition pursuits. Here are all the major professional roles you will need to fill, keep in mind that an individual or firm may perform one or more of these roles.

1. The business broker or investment banker for deal sourcing
2. The Transaction accountants for financial due diligence
3. The Tax accountants for deal structuring and tax due diligence
4. The Valuation advisor for independent value determination and assessment
5. The legal team for legal representations, warranties and reviews
6. The human resources and benefits consultants for personnel matters
7. The IT consultants for technology related integration issues
8. The financing advisor/banker for deal financing arrangements
9. The deal Coach for general coaching and support system for the business owner

Planning for and pulling this team together in preparation for an growth stacking is the most important and critical thing that the most savvy of entrepreneurs do. The deal team is the mastermind for every successful acquisition and literally makes or breaks the entire process.

The Team

You are the quarterback in these deals, you call the shots and your team of experts get it done. You are the leader of the team and they execute your plays, so you need to be very familiar with what plays to call and when. This is one reason that you'll want to start with smaller deals

> **Never, Ever, Ever attempt an acquisition without a properly constituted deal team, this is a team effort!**

first and then as your plays get better and you get more sophisticated you can more easily pursue larger acquisitions. Just like any other business activity, acquisitions are team-based with each expert covering the bases in their own turf. The lack of this understanding is what discourages most business owners to engage acquisition as a growth tool. The team exists to accomplish the goal together and success in the process is a collective effort.

The critical milestone at this point is to establish and communicate a strategic objective to the team of the plan to acquire businesses within your established priorities and criteria that the deal team is fully aware of and understand.

This process was a fantastically expensive education for me. Going through this I learned everything from the most expensive and highly paid teachers, my highly paid advisers. Because every question I had was answered by a highly paid, highly educated professional while I was in the middle of negotiating this closing. Such as when I found out the advantages and disadvantages of asset sales versus stock sales and the tremendous tax implications each type of sale had. I've learned that by paying a specialized tax lawyer to teach me this. But without his advice, without him there to teach me I would have never even known which questions to ask. But through this experience all of the pieces of the puzzle were revealed to me and I learned the hard way, the expensive way, the best strategic ways to buy and sell a business. So, having someone there to coach me and guide me would have been a tremendous cost savings to me and I would have gained much more strategic knowledge on the front end of this deal

There will be deals that don't go through and there will be negotiations that end after the first meeting. But even if you decide not to close on a deal, it is wise to assess the strengths and weaknesses of your own organization as well as those of the target company relative to the opportunity. You'll be able to see what you are doing better than other businesses or what others are not doing right and how they can be improved, if those businesses were owned by you. This process alone can give you a rare opportunity to have a free look-inside to other businesses.

As I mentioned in the previous sections, the business that purchased my company was much more savvy at business acquisitions than I was. They had done this many, many more times than I had so they were truly focused on what was going to happen after the sale closed. As the negotiations progressed and as the due diligence got underway if they had offered me some type of long-term buyout I think I would have accepted it because as long as I was able to meet my own personal long-term goals which was my personal financial security I would have accepted a deal that met those objectives. It would have certainly had to make sure that it made sense to me but I certainly would have considered any other options that would have met my goals. It would have made the deal more complex because I would have built in securities in the closing documents that made sure that I was compensated fairly for long-term buyout. The reason I think telling you about this is important is because that many entrepreneurs think that the only deal that they will accept will be an all cash offer without giving serious consideration to their long-term financial goals first and then entertaining any offer that met these goals.   I know this

---

because this is exactly what I went through and I know that if the deal was structured correctly I would've accepted any offer that met my long-term family financial goals. This also reminds me of how in 2008 video was becoming a great tool for sales and production in my industry. So, instead of learning all of the details necessary to start a video production department within my company, I actually purchased a video sales production company. This was an all cash deal, but the integration of a completely different company would have never been able to be accomplished had I not had all of the business systems documentation completed. So these two examples were totally different reasons for acquiring companies and it does come down to making sure that financing of the deal could have been accomplished in multiple different ways as well as the integration of the two companies can be done in many different ways.

What's the Target Worth?

Once you have made contact, and the expression of your interest in a company that fits your criteria is accepted, valuing the business you are now considering buying becomes a key concern. You definitely don't want to overpay. However if you are unrealistic in your expectations and you persistently try to negotiate for a bargain basement price you may find yourself spinning your wheels as seller after seller concludes that you are not a serious buyer. I know may entrepreneurs that have lost out on an acquisitions of great businesses because they tried to avoid paying the extra $15,000 the seller was demanding for at closing. These are hard fought lessons and show many entrepreneurs that price is just only one of the important elements in an acquisition decision and not always the most important decision.

Figuring out what a business is worth isn't as precise a process as you might want it to be. There is no secret pricing formula, no expert estimate, or clairvoyant that can provide you with just the right figure. The essence of the valuation processes is so you can arrive at a reasonable price range that you will use in your negotiation with the seller.

What happens so often is that sellers get caught up in getting to a number that they think their business is worth and much less thought is given to what they are trying to accomplish after the sale. So my own personal reasons for selling the business played a large role in determining the price of the business. I wanted to make sure that after the business was sold I had financial security with really conservative investing because security of my investment was more important than growth since I've was only 42 years old when I sold the company. The sale of this business had to take care of me for the rest of my life, God willing another 40 years! In my case personally, the investing 4% thumb rule was what I used to determine my selling price by working backwards from what I needed to support my lifestyle after the business sale was completed. So as long as the business sale price met my long-term financial objectives I knew I could be flexible with my price. This was combined with the uniqueness I created in my business and made sure that it was a great fit for my buyers in multiple ways. One way was the unique marketing system I had in place, unique in this industry anyway. Another way was the rapid growth the company had just experienced and timing played a role in making the company unique because of this. So I was able to get closer to a 7X multiplier of earnings roughly as a selling price for the company and that amount fit in perfectly with my long-term financial goals.

The valuation process also helps you to evaluate your ability to pay for what you are trying to buy. This doesn't mean that you must have the entire cash component on hand, or even that your company must make the subsequent payment from its own cash flow. There are a wide variety of ways acquisition payments can be financed and made, including contributions from the acquired business itself.

To establish an appropriate purchase price for an acquisition, start by compiling detailed historical financial and projected financial results for the target company (the reliability should be verified through detailed financial due diligence, as well as for your own experience in business operation. These projections should include all the economies of scale that might accrue from the operation of the target as a part of your company, or other savings you might realize in a corporate rather than individual owner environment. In addition, any working capital contributions or short-term capital equipment needs of the target should also be considered. These are as much as part of the purchase price as the cash paid at closing.

> Are you ready to take the next logical step? Schedule your contractor market assessment. So you can identify the prospects that are 600 X more likely to turn into a new customer…and it's FREE too!
> Simply go to www. MEERScore.com/freeoffer and fill out the application for a 45 minute phone call with Mike Layton.
>
> As a special bonus, this includes an additional FREE strategy session to get your customized plan for exponential growth with Walter Bergeron.

Valuation Approaches

The three major methods used in arriving at the value for businesses for sale are:

1. The Asset-Based Approach: This involves tallying up the value of the assets, starting with the tangible ones, such as furniture, equipment and inventory – using resale rather than replacement numbers. The figure you arrive at will probably be the smallest amount the seller will accept for a business. But, if you are looking at a money-losing or otherwise troubled business – or if the seller is under pressure to quickly sell a tiny business that depends primarily on the seller's efforts – then the value of the physical assets may be the most the seller can hope to get and should be the most you are willing to pay.

Even a business that's been performing poorly may be worth more than the value of its tangible assets. For example, the business may have favorable long-term contracts with customers or suppliers or other intangible assets that translate into additional value. Similarly, the seller may be able to demonstrate that there is value in a business name or in patents, copyrights or customer lists the business own. Employees too, can be an important intangible asset. In contrast, negative factors such as unresolved lawsuits can reduce its value.

Business liabilities, whether known or unknown will be significant only if you'll be assuming responsibility for them. If the seller agrees to be solely responsible – and you are convinced that the seller has the financial resources to follow through – the liabilities are unlikely to affect the asset pricing of a business.

2. The Income Valuation Approach: This method assumes that you're looking at a business as just one more type of investment, competing for your resources with stocks, bonds, real estate and other business opportunities. The key question then becomes, 'What kind of return would you expect from an investment in this business?' Once you arrive at that number. You can then work backward to determine the price you are willing to pay. This method also assumes that you won't buy a business that doesn't give you the return you want on your investment. Rather than determining what the business is worth on some objective level, this method helps you determine what the business is worth to you, given what you hope to accomplish by purchasing it.

Here is how it works:
   Business Value = Expected Annual Profits / Desired Rate of Return
   What this means is that if a business is earning $100,000 per year and you expect that business to represent a 10% return on your investment. What that then means is that

---

for you to pay for a business that is going to be producing 10% return to you then you wouldn't pay more than $1 million for that business. Because you're expected rate of return determines the amount of money you'll be investing in that business.

If you are seeking a conservative investment, you might look into U.S. government bonds. The money you invest in that bond is considered safe. But most any business is more risky than U.S. government bonds or other conservative investment. So if you are looking to buy a business as an investment, you'll reasonably want your expected annual rate of return to be higher, at times at least three times the return on U.S government bonds in order to compensate for the higher risks.

Before you use the income formula however, you need to be convinced that you can predict the business profits for the next three to five years with a reasonable degree of accuracy. Otherwise, you have nothing solid on which to base your computations – it's all speculation. Also, the rate of return you expect to receive is crucial. However, it neglects the impact of future inflation or deflation on the business and its income. More important is the fact you won't be looking at the business as mere investment but as growth addition to your existing business. The associated integration issues need to be considered as well beyond the dollars and cents.

3. The Comparable Company Sales: The value of recently concluded business sales could provide information on how to price a potential acquisition, especially those similar to them. For this approach, the most useful information from recent sales are usually the multiples of sales, earnings or EBITDA (earnings, before, interest, tax, depreciation and amortization), which is used as a proxy for cash flow. The relationship between the price paid for the completed transactions and the key value drivers like sales, earnings, and cash flow of the sold companies can help in determining an estimate of value for the potential transaction. The limitation of this approach is that you may not have access to the other important details that are part of the closed transaction.

The other challenge in using this approach is that there may be few, if any, recent sales of similar businesses. Also because small businesses tend to be unique, even a business that's similar on the surface probably won't be the same as the one you are considering: location, sales volume, number of employees, and a host of other important factors can make comparison difficult.

Despite the difficulties with comparable sales, if you're able to use information from a number of sources, including trade publications, business brokers, the internet, and personal contacts, you should be able to come up with a reasonably accurate ballpark estimate for what businesses like the one you are considering to buy could be settled for.

Other Approaches:

In addition to the generally adopted methods, the following two approaches are also used in small business transactions. So you may need to familiarize yourself with them:

A. Industry Formulas and Rules of Thumb – in some specific areas of business, such as bakeries, tax services, and publishing, certain valuation formulas have gained credence. For example, you might discover that there is a held belief that a certain type of business commonly sells for ten times profits or two times sales. Unquestionably, such formulas promise a quick and easy way to price a business. The problem is that these formulas are almost always too simplistic to serve as anything more than a very rough guide for the sale of real businesses, with their quirks and characteristics.

B. Formulas Based on Sales or Earnings – In some industries, sales values are arrived at by multiplying either gross sales or net earnings by a number that's generally accepted in that business community. In theory, these formulas are derived from industry over a number of years, as represented by data covering a lot of previous sales. In reality, such formulas may be based on little more than industry lore and may not accurately reflect current market conditions or the particular business niche you are in.

So if you are considering buying a business in a field where formulas like this are part of the culture, go ahead and look at what the figure would be using the formula. But then make sure you carefully consider all of the factors that might cause the sale price to deviate from the number you reach with that calculation. And be prepared for the seller to do the same.

Range of Value

Once determined, the purchase price range, depending on the business, on the low end will probably be little more than the liquidation value of the physical assets. The high end is likely to be based on income projections, and what you think is reasonable to pay for the right to receive (and hopefully increase) those earnings in the future.

If the business is healthy, especially with a well-established customer base, positive reputation and well documented operating system, the seller would probably start the negotiations by stating an asking price toward the top of the range of possible values for that business but may back off a bit in negotiating the final price.

Factors Affecting Value

Regardless of the valuation model used, keep in mind that your resultant numbers are at best guestimates: there are other important factors that influence the worth of a business and what you as a buyer are willing to pay for it.

The key factors include:

1. **Terms of Payment:** the price you pay is often tied directly to the terms of payment, such as the amount of down payment, the repayment period and the interest rate. All of these can affect what you are willing to pay and what the seller is willing to accept. For example, if you'll be paying for the business over five years rather than three, the seller may insist on charging you more because of the longer lasting risk that you'll default. And you may be willing to pay a bit more for the privilege of lower payments and a longer payment period. Similarly, paying 100% cash at closing for the business may also significantly alter the final price. Though I won't advise it!

2. **Market Demand:** as in the purchase of anything of value, including business, the state of current demand affects price. The timing of the sale could exert upward or downward pressure on the price: many similar businesses on the market, factory closings may indicate a slowing economy. What other buyers may be willing to pay for what the seller has to sell will exert influence on you for what you will eventually pay: though as a savvy business person you must independently figure out a realistic bottom line for buying any business as an investment – your analysis must have shown you not just what the business might be worth in terms of its fair market value, but also your clarity as to what you, specifically are willing or can afford to pay for it.

3. **Seller's Personal Needs or Preferences:** there are situations outside of the business condition that may force a seller to sell a business quickly, within months, or possibly even weeks of making the decision to sell. If for reason of poor health, financial pressures, divorce or other personal matters a seller needs to sell quickly, you may be able to acquire the business at much less than the top dollar the seller might otherwise have been able to command. Other situation includes seller's unwillingness to work for you during the transition period due to pressing personal matters.

Please note: These types of situations provide unique buying opportunities that may provide great upsides for value hunters. You should give priority to seeking these kinds of opportunities. Understanding the seller's motivation for selling will enable you to understand whether it falls under a fast and quick doable deal or the seller is not highly motivated to sell and may be adamant about his or her asking price.

1. **Type of Opportunity:** Depending on your buying perspective for a particular acquisition opportunity, the price you are willing to pay will be impacted. For example, if an opportunity is unsolicited and you wanted to minimize your invested resources, you may low-ball the seller. However, if you are buying the business as a strategic addition to your existing business, and know that you can reap the benefit of scale quickly, you may be willing to pay more for it, knowing that you'll earn it back through increased profits in the next few years.

2. **Sales of Comparable Businesses:** a common way for setting value on a business is checking out what similar businesses have sold for. That is looking at 'comparables' or 'comps.' The information may be incomplete though, given the transactions are usually confidential and certain terms may be unique to the transaction being evaluated.

So the price paid for similar businesses tend to influence the range of value the parties in another transaction may negotiate around.

Do The Deal Techniques

A properly constituted deal team will address all the essential and technical facets of an acquisition. The team would also ensure that the acquisition can pay for itself by helping to organize for traditional financing through bank loans and other similar traditional sources.

The major area where savvy deal-makers extract additional value upfront is in the area of leveraged acquisitions strategies commonly described as little or no money down techniques.

1. Flexible Sellers: Usually large corporations disposing off a subsidiary, sellers selling their businesses due to illness, death, forced retirement, divorce or unforeseen emergencies that were unprepared for, are open to deal structures offering quick sale. This situation could allow the business to be paid for in installments with little or no cash upfront.

2. Large Fixed Assets Owned: A business that has huge fixed assets offers great opportunity for asset-based lenders to provide funding for the acquirer to use the assets of the business in raising financing to acquire it. What this means is that you are basically using the assets of the business to pay for the business.

3. High Customer and Trade Receivable Balances: Like fixed assets, receivables could be monetized through factoring to raise financing for acquiring a business.

4. High Cash-Generating Businesses: The consistent high cash flow pattern could be used to secure short-term financing to fund the down payment.

5. High Cash and Bank Balances: They can be used to secure short-term loans for meeting down-payment requirements, and utilized upon closing to pay the loans off. In other words when you are looking at a business financials and you see that a business a high cash balance you can actually leverage that cash balance as a means of securing a short-term loan with your existing banker with the understanding that upon closing that cash in the target company can be used to pay off the loan.

6. Excess Inventory or Unnecessary Stockpile: If the business has inventory you do not want – or even if it has inventory that is desirable but in excess – you can sell off this unneeded inventory prior to and contingent upon buying the business.

7. Multi-divisions or Products Business: Unrelated divisions or product-lines that is different from the ones you currently have you can dispose of those product lines or divisions to raise financing.

8. Assumable Trade or Notes Payables: These could be assumed to reduce total payments due to seller.

9. Mismanaged or Underperforming Business: This offers opportunity for low acquisition value and flexible payment terms; and could be a typical diamond-in-the rough once the leadership is changed. Because when a business is struggling, either because it does not understand the systems that these blueprints share in phases one and two. With a well-established marketing system and a business that is running on autopilot you are able to buy a struggling business for cheap and be in the position to turn around quickly period

10. Adjusted Tax Advantage: Where there is a significant difference between the tax adjusted and accounting values of assets, the transaction could be structured through the purchase price allocation that would make the purchase an attractive acquisition.

11. Unexpired Loss Carried Over: They could be very valuable in shielding future tax obligations.

Now that you have valued the business and the seller is motivated one important area that has been a key issue for most acquirers is what we have termed smart acquisition financing and structuring.

Smart Acquisition Financing & Structuring

Once the price is agreed upon, its payment methods should be based on the target's historical financial results. The price should then be balanced against the excepted cash flow from the combined operations and all debt service requirements for both. Although most sellers contend that their company will grow and profits will increase, you should never pay for the future in advance. If appropriate to the transaction, there are ways to reward a seller for future results that didn't involve a higher initial purchase price.

Once you have calculated a price that you feel is appropriate for the acquisition, focus the negotiations more on the methods of making the payments to the seller than on the price itself. Although that is not always possible, the payment methods can often make a higher price feasible, and can therefore be used to bridge a gap between what a seller feels his company is worth and what a buyer can afford to pay. In other words when you look at a business and given the skills that you have acquired through the marketing system and the business automation system that was discussed previously you can see how you can quickly turn a struggling business into a cash- generating machine. The key here is not to just focus on the lowest price you buy the company for, but on what you're going to do with the business and the ability to be able to turn the corner and being able to offer the business for sale in a much easier and better way.

As a buyer, it is absolutely important that you ensure that all required payments can be made without damaging either the parent company or the original objectives of the acquisition. This means that you must carefully analyze each component of the purchase price and the funding sources that might be available for each. For a simple transaction with cash payment at closing plus a note to be held by the seller, this analysis should focus on a calculation of the debt service coverage.

This coverage ratio includes the payment obligations for all elements of the acquisition funding, all other short-term and long-term debts of the combined companies, and any required working capital and capital equipment contributions. So, when you're looking at the acquisition you want to see the impact of the purchase on your future cash flow. You don't want to buy the business and realize that you are going to have to sacrifice the operating cash from your existing business and not be able to fund or finance the payment arrangements you have made with the seller. You want to be seen in the industry as a dealmaker who complies with all terms of the deal he has made. These payments are then compared with a realistic projection of cash flow from the combined operations. Conservatively, the total debt service coverage by quarter during the first year should be no less than 2-to-1; though in certain situations with unusually stable earnings in well-understood markets, 1.5-to-1 could be acceptable. After the first year though, the debt service coverage ratio should increase significantly.

Importance of Liquidity

In assessing an acquisition and its price, don't forget, money is the blood – when it stops flowing, you are dead.

Before embarking on an acquisition, carefully assess your appetite for risk, and even more carefully calculate the ability of the combined operations to pay for the acquisition. Once you have signed and closed the transaction the biggest challenges now are integrating the two businesses.

Managing Post-Acquisition Integration

Despite the potential problems you identify during the initial priorities and criteria stages, most transactions fail because of the lack of ability or sufficient management talent to support the acquisition, monitor its progress, and control its operations. That is, the inability to manage what you buy, which is critically essential for successful and smart acquisition pursuits.

To avoid this problem, carefully evaluate a potential acquisition in the light of the strength and weaknesses of its operating systems and your existing operations. Look closely at the principal corporate functions (leadership, sales, accounting, administration, and other relevant areas) the people you have managing each area and the people overseeing these functions in the target company.

Upon the completion of the deal, the major tasks involve merging functions with the acquired company and making required changes to it in order to ensure that the identified pre-deal investment benefits are achieved.

Managing the acquired companies is not difficult, but it is different. A higher level of skill is required, along with a more complete system of internal controls. The success or failure of any acquisition will depend to a great extent upon the management talent available in both companies, the authority given to those managers, and the **Never, Ever, Ever attempt an acquisition without a properly constituted deal team, this is a team effort!** financial and other tools provided to them to do their jobs and to gauge their own performances. Addressing these management issues should be done before closing an acquisition, not after; though the execution starts when both companies come together.

Working With The Pro's

As you can see, buying a business requires a plethora of diverse skills. It is like a typical team sport that needs to work together seamlessly. Each team member needs to be clear as to what they are responsible for and to what extent.

Before you start the process of looking for a business to buy, and then move into negotiating and closing a deal, you will need to decide how much of the work you want to delegate to others and how much you are prepared to do yourself (using your in-house personnel).

If your purchase is fairly straightforward and you want to limit expenses, you may decide to perform many routine tasks yourself, using occasional expert help from a lawyer, an accountant or perhaps a business broker to provide the professional vetting for many of the tasks in the acquisition process (including sample documents provided in this blueprint). But to make this approach work, you will need to find professionals who are willing to offer advise, serve as objective sounding boards, and do some technical chores without trying to take over the whole job.

However, you may need more than occasional professional help (the subcontracting model) and rely more heavily on professional assistance, doing little if anything yourself, under the following circumstances:

1. You have never bought a business before
2. You are buying a business from a sophisticated seller who is aided by a team of seasoned professionals. Just like Walter shared, his buyers came with a slew of seasoned professionals while he had to start looking for his team after they had already contacted him.
3. You anticipate there will be unusual legal or financial complexities that go beyond ordinary business activities.

4. The deal involves a substantial amount of money you wan to make sure that the terms and conditions in the agreement do not expose you to potential liabilities.
5. You are buying a business that owns – and will be transferring to you – real estate or significant intellectual property.
6. You are unsure about the best way to include co-buyers or other parties in your transaction. Because some of the doable deal opportunities we listed in the blueprints may require you even having other investors invest with you in the business with the understanding that at some point in the future you will be a will to buy them out. You will need seasoned professionals to help you structure this type of deal.

Nevertheless, always remember that you are responsible for every decision. The professionals are only on the deal to support you in making the best decisions for you! You call the shots!!

Are you ready to take the next logical step? Schedule your contractor market assessment. So you can identify the prospects that are 600 X more likely to turn into a new customer…and it's FREE too!
Simply go to www. MEERScore.com/freeoffer and fill out the application for a 45 minute phone call with Mike Layton.

As a special bonus, this includes an additional FREE strategy session to get your customized plan for exponential growth with Walter Bergeron.

Paying For The Deal Team

Now, the good thing about being a business owner is that you already have a network of professionals you work with. These are the same people you used as part of your deal team as well as who you used as sources of potential companies to buy. Now what you will need to have a formal discussion with them. The discussion will go like this: You can see that we been doing very well in the last two or three years, now we are thinking about buying other businesses. These businesses or going to come in different sizes and shapes and we may have to look at 10 or 20 of them. Would you be open to only charging us when the transaction closes by keeping open a work in progress file for us. When a transaction closes we'll include your charges as a cost that is part of acquiring the business. When a transaction does not close, we will agree that as the business continues to grow you will become the accountant or the auditor of the business, we'll do business exclusively with you. In my experience 4 out of 10 times they will say yes to this deal structure. Why? Because every professional does what is called business development. So the $250 an hour for the work you they do for you in the course of acquisitions that do not work out can will be discounted with the understanding that when the deal does close we can add that to the transaction. This means when the transaction does close those fees they become part of your cost of operating the business.

Chapter 7

Get Out While The Getting's Good

Now there are literally hundreds, if not thousands, of different ways and variations to exit your business and it is really easy to get overwhelmed with all the options available to you. But, this exit is all about making sure you sell your business for the most amount of money you can possibly get for it with a single sale. That type of exit is done with what I call the Profit Stacking Exit.

Profit Stacking Exit

So let's get to it shall we. The Profit Stacking Exit is very similar to the Growth Stacking process you used when looking to grow your business. The priorities and criteria you used to select target acquisitions works in reverse when it comes time to sell your company. The Profit Stacking Exit has 3 major components to it. The first component is the Right Buyer, step one is to find out who is the right buyer for your business and compile a list of who those potential buyers are. Once you determine the who, things start to fall into place much faster and easier for you.

> You will be looking for a buyer that can turn this acquisition into exponential growth for themselves too.

You will be looking for a buyer that can turn this acquisition into exponential growth for themself too, so that even if they paid you full retail asking price for your business it'll still be a bargain. When you show them the potential growth they can achieve then when they acquire your company, then any price becomes a bargain. Any amount they pay you for your business will be well worth it because their return on investment will far outweigh the cost. Here is who is going to be the right buyer for your exit to have the largest potential profit level.

Proactive Buyer Selection

You pick the buyer, the buyer does not pick you. You will always be involved in actively searching for the perfect buyer for your company. Just as you did with actively searching for the best client for your products and services you will now actively search for the best client to buy your company. You must be aware that during every interaction you have with another company, you should be thinking about whether or not this company would benefit from owning your company. Your buyer will be a strategic buyer that can use Growth Stacking to build his business just as you used it in yours. So when you interact with your suppliers, you should ask yourself this question. "Would this company be able to buy my company and use Growth Stacking to grow their company exponentially?" When you interact with your clients, ask yourself this question. "Would this company be able to buy my company and use Growth Stacking to grow their company exponentially?" When you interact with any other type of business owners at public or private functions, you should be asking yourself, "Would this company be able to buy my company and use Growth Stacking to grow their company exponentially?" Make yourself a list of every interaction you currently have with another company and go through that list and ask yourself the question. "Would this company be able to buy my company and use Growth Stacking to grow their company exponentially?" Now you have the start of a list of potential buyers.

Now in looking at who is right to buy your company I had the pleasure of doing some work with GKIC former CEO Bette Tomaszevich and she shared some wonderful strategies. She bought an educational company and built it up quite large, many millions of dollars. And she knew that she was always going to sell the company at some point and that the right buyer was going to be one of her customers. Her advice to me was to always have in mind who you are going to sell the business to, always be looking for that person to sell it to.

She was always looking for potential buyers and she would build the business in ways that would help her to strategically place the business in the best position to be purchased by that type of company. One of her larger customers was the best and most strategic type of company to acquire her company. So on many occasions she would start getting business from a new customer and then start leading the CEO into conversations about acquisition. Sometimes if the conversation got to that point she would actually show them the path to acquiring her company. Lot's of times they were not interested in acquisitions as a method of expansion, but there were a few that were, so don't get discouraged by someone telling you no. But, eventually she ran across a large client that had done previous acquisitions and recognized what she was talking about in her conversations. They eventually bought her company in large part due to her steering many conversations in that direction. Now she certainly didn't start off the conversations with "Hey do you want to buy my company" but she started off by feeling them out if they had even done an acquisition and recognized the power of expansion and growth through acquisitions.

I did a very similar thing when I started talks with my eventual buyer. Once I got the idea to sell my company I began many conversations with my vendors as well as my customers about potential acquisitions. It turned out that many of them had done acquisitions and that if the deal that I eventually accepted had not gone through I had multiple back up deals to pursue. And so it's a great way to get involved with a potential buyer by showing them the path to a purchase of your company.

Proactive Buyer Elimination

Who you are not going to sell the business to is just as important as selecting who you are going to be able to sell the business too. It's very easy to waste a lot of time looking at the wrong buyers, so let's eliminate who you will not even consider to sell the business to as a general rule.

With only very rare exceptions, in order to maximize the sales amount, you will want to sell your business to another company, not an individual.

You will not be selling your business to any of your competitors, because you will want to show your buyer how they will benefit from owning you and one of the ways you will show that your company is worth so much money is by employing Growth Stacking and that is the Cross Selling Multiplier. In order for the Cross Selling Multiplier technique to be useful to you now, your buyer must have a complimentary product or service, it cannot be a competitive service or this technique doesn't work as well to your advantage. So, no competitors!

For the Cross Marketing Multiplier to work your buyer must have a complimentary product or service.

Complimentary Product or Service

This is a continuation of why you don't want to sell to your competitors. You want your buyer to have the advantage of being able to grow using the Cross Marketing Multiplier, so give this some real thought. When looking at your clients, look at all of the other products and services that they buy. All of these are potential sources of buyer companies for your business. When you were doing your research on companies you might buy, that list will also serve you as potential company types that might be a good buyer for your company. Take another look at the list you came up with for your priorities and criteria and use these as a starting place for the types of companies that would be a great fit to buy you out.

Identical Client Type

When looking at the buyer pool you want to find a buyer that your company will be of the greatest benefit to. So the company must have identical clients as yours, but ideally no overlap. So when we mentioned just a minute ago that every interaction with other businesses you should ask yourself a question of whether or not this company would benefit from owning my company. One of the criteria that you should consider very important is do they have the same type of clients as you do. This plays into the strategy of the Cross Marketing Multiplier from the Growth Stacking process.

Similar Size

You will want to select businesses that are of similar or a little larger size than you are, as large as 10 times your size but no more. The reason for this is because you want to be able to show the buyer not just in money terms but also in multiplier terms just how much growth they can achieve by strategically acquiring your company, as well as show them a short timeframe for a full return on their investment. So for example: If you sold your company for $10 million, you could show them a path to a $50 million growth of their company in 3 years by using the Growth Stacking process. To another $10 million dollar company this would be phenomenal growth and they will likely have never thought about having this type of growth level through any other means. Even to a $100 million company a $50 million growth over 3 years is still phenomenal. But as the company size continues to get larger you won't be able to show them as a large of a growth and then your business value to them and the price they are willing to pay is not as significant to them. So, unless you get an offer you can't refuse, stick to companies in the sweet spot size of 1 to 10 times as large as your company for now.

Solution Fit

Just as when you acquired other companies with problems that you had solutions to, you must have a solution to the buyer's problem. This may sound obvious, but make sure that you have at least one really outstanding unique solution to a problem of your buyer. One of two common problems that usually exist is a poor marketing system and poor systematization of business processes. Since you have already seen how to implement both of those solutions into your business you will have those solutions in your pocket and be able to offer them to your buyer as a unique and tremendously valuable asset.

Problem Fit

You must have a big problem that the buyer has the solution for. Now, I know what you're thinking, you're thinking that you don't ever want to knowingly tell a potential buyer that your business has problems, but you do. The fact is that every business has problems and they are going to be discovered during the due diligence process anyway, so the best thing to do is to use your weaknesses to your advantage. This sounds a bit counterintuitive but follow me for a second. Let's say that your business has a good sales department but it's small, only 2 or 3 sales reps. So, your problem is that you have a limited size sales department and if you had 10 sales reps, your sales would skyrocket. So the problem of limited sales force has a solution another company can easily solve by having a larger, more well-trained sales force. Your job will be to make this well known and point out to the prospective buyer that your weakness is their strength and that the solution is easy and quick and plays to their advantage.

Proactive Offer Seeking

Armed with a list of potential buyers, you are now going to use Proactive Offer Seeking to design an offer package, implement a marketing campaign and go out there and solicit offers for your business. Now this is done in phases starting with the potential buyers that you have the best relationship with.

Segment your buyer list by breaking it into 3 categories. Category one is those businesses you have a relationship with. Category two is those businesses that you have any type of connection with, such as through an association or friend of a friend or any type of common ground that you can easily start off a conversation with. Category three is those businesses that you have no connection to at all.

Low hanging fruit

Starting with category one, the potential buyers you already have a relationship with. You will call them directly and ask for an in person meeting with them. You will meet with each of them and explain that you are exiting the business and then give them a copy of the offer package.

Higher Hanging Fruit

With category two buyers you are going to get a tighter relationship with them by again making calls to set up phone appointments and speak to them about your proposal and ask them to set up in person meetings. If they accept then you'll do the same thing as the low hanging fruit and meet with them and leave an offer package with them.

Highest Hanging Fruit

With category three buyers you will begin with the investigation process of who it is you need to talk to then follow the steps laid out previously to begin a conversation. The marketing campaign is designed to make sure that you make your initial contact in a warm way so make sure you don't skimp on the marketing follow-up process.

Offer Package Creation

This is the package you will use to deliver your message of why your prospective buyer should buy your company and here are the parts you'll need:

Introduction – Who you are, how long you have been in business, what your products and services are. This will give them a good general idea of who you are. Now there are different schools of thought on how much information to share at this point. In my opinion the more you feel comfortable with sharing, the better, but get your team involved with determining how much detail you want to go into here.

<u>Show them the Path</u> - This is just a preliminary detailed explanation of what they could do with a company like yours and show them the pathway of exponential growth. Yep, you're going to show them how much they could potentially earn and how quickly they could earn it by buying you out and that if they bought you out at any price it would be a bargain. This is the part of the package that often gets left out, but is super critical because it's so power. This gives your prospect the reason to buy your company and what sets you apart from any alternative, including doing nothing at all. This even works when they are not considering acquisitions at this time because what you are explaining to them is so valuable that they won't want to pass on this opportunity.

<u>Price Juxtaposition</u> – Show them how much money it would cost them to achieve this on their own and tell them how long it would take without an acquisition. This sets the bar high so that when they find out your asking price, it'll be much lower.

<u>Call to Action</u> – Tell them that the next step is to submit an offer OR contact you or your broker with further questions or concerns.

<u>Deadline</u> – Give them 2 weeks to take the next step and contact you to be put on the list for consideration as a potential buyer. Get with your team here too to make sure the timeframe for a deadline is appropriate to your situation.

<u>Prepare your offer</u> – This is really about preparing a marketing package to give to potential buyers, this explains to them the biggest benefits to them. This is not a list of your assets and then telling them a price. At this point you are not going to tell them how much you are asking. You end the package with a form explaining to them that you are entertaining offers and leave an opening for further conversations to cover any questions or concerns.

Team – You will need to have your team take a look at the offers, this is not something you want to do on your own. Get your team on board to guide you through this step and never go beyond this step without your deal team fully aware of what's going on.

Marketing Campaign

I hope you realize what you have just accomplished with this exercise and what you have just done for yourself. If you recall back in the marketing chapter, I went over the direct marketing results triangle. I covered the message, the market and the media. Well, you just selected the market through your buyer selection process. You just came up with a unique message by showing your buyer the path to exponential growth and you selected one part of your media with the offer package. Now would be a good time to use the marketing chapter to select the best media to reach your target market. At the very least, this will be a multiple step campaign using multiple media types.

Pawn Stars

I am a big fan of a show on the history channel called Pawn Stars. If you are unfamiliar with the show it's about a family run pawn shop and people come in and mostly sell their stuff to the pawn shop. It's kept interesting by one of the family members named Rick Harrison. As an aside he's got a great book about his pawn shop called License to Pawn, great book and quite interesting story about how he and his dad got into the business. So anyway, I have seen this happen on numerous occasions that someone will come in to pawn some antique gun for instance and typically I notice it's an elderly little old lady and one of the first questions Rick usually asks is "How much do you want for it?" Now in most cases the customer wants way too much for it, and Rick talks them down and gives them a realistic value for what they've got, but on occasion and as I mention I notice that's it's always the little old lady, well she wants way too little. She thinks it's worth like $500 bucks and Rick can tell at a glance that she's got some genuine heirloom and it's worth like many thousands of dollars. But, and this is something what I love about Rick is that he's basically an honest guy, now I don't know if it's just because she's a frail little old lady or why it is, but Rick will tell her that it's worth way more than what she wants and he will give her more than she asked for it. And this is probably one of the perks to being a little old lady, people are generally genuine and honest.

Now to the contrast I have seen other Pawn store owners come in and know exactly what they have and exactly what it's worth and they will tell Rick almost down to the penny how much they want for it but then they also tell Rick things like, you have the perfect clients to buy this from you and here's how much profit you're gonna' make off of it and here's how long before you'll make that profit. And on more than one occasion I've seen Rick give them exactly how much they asked for, no haggling, no bargaining, just shake hands and go do the paperwork.

Rick Harrison Won't Buy Your Business

What I want to say is that when it comes time to sell your business you cannot be that little old lady because Rick Harrison is not going to be buying your business and I can guarantee you that 99.99999% of the time the guy sitting across the negotiating table that wants to buy your company is NOT going to tell you that it's worth more than you are asking. He's going to haggle with you no matter how much you ask for it. You need to be like the other pawn shop owner and tell the buyer exactly what they're going to get, how much profit they are going to make and how long it's going to take them to make it and then and only then are you going to be able to get the top dollar value for your business. The value of your business is just as much based on physical assets as it is based on the vision of how the company is going to profit the buyer and that vision can be shown to the buyer by you or you can rely on the buyer to visualize it on his own. Now, which choice do you want to chose, do you want to rely on the buyer to see all the possibilities or do you think it would be better if you, based on your experience with your business, can show the buyer in great detail all the possibilities.

Now, the way you know how to do this is for the first thing it would be extremely helpful if you have been a buyer first and know what's happening on both sides of that negotiating table. And secondly, you better know exactly what you've got to offer and why the buyer is interested in buying it so you can position yourself and show off the most important reasons they should buy your company. This is really about marketing your business properly for sale. You should know who your buyer is, you should know what their frustrations are, you should be able to picture who this person and company is that are going to be the best type of buyer for your company.

Savvy entrepreneurs never get involved in a venture without contemplating upfront, their exit plan! It would be like going into a building without knowing the way out. All the sweat and labor you put into the business would have amounted to nothing if your exit is done as an accident that you didn't plan for.

These savvy entrepreneurs start planning an exit strategy the day they start their businesses. Their businesses are chosen carefully, knowing that someday they will want to sell that business at a substantial profit. They know the industry they choose to do business in, inside-out, in order to run it – and sell it – successfully.

Sell It From The Start

In other words, the most successful businesses are built to sell from the onset. The business owner has been building an exit pathway for himself while developing the processes, procedures and automating the operation for growth. That growth is done organically through direct

---

marketing, exponentially through acquisitions or the most savvy of the savvy entrepreneurs do both. They grow organically as well as exponentially through acquisitions. Now, I know what you are going to say. You are going to say that buying other companies is way out of my league and that this is not for me. But I want to assure you that acquiring other companies to meet your growth goals can be done in a business of any size in order to maximize the value available at the exit and even get businesses just like yours to the $10 million dollar level. This is especially true in blue-collar businesses like mine was in the industrial sector, it can be done for HVAC companies, mechanical contractors, electrical industries, plumbing, piping, manufacturing, I even have a client doing it with a wire rope and sling distribution company. Any blue-collar business is prime to grow through acquisitions, even yours. It can even be done without any money, but that's a topic for another conversation, let's focus now on the exit strategy.

An exit strategy stresses the need for you to begin with the end in mind as you build that business. In other words, when you are thinking of how you build your business, you also have to ask yourself: "Why am I doing everything I am doing?" Because if your goal is to sell the company so you can live life with 100% financial freedom and 100% time freedom, then you must structure your business in a way that it will be able to serve you until the day you die. But more importantly, you also have to ask yourself: "What happens to my family?" "What happens to the people who are working for me and helping me realize my life's goal?" An exit strategy is what will help you to create a system that will enable you cash out the value you have been creating all these years.

> An exit strategy stresses the need for you to begin with the end in mind as you build your business.

Many times entrepreneurs don't begin with the end in mind, typically it's not in our nature. We begin with the journey in mind. We begin there because we are looking for the thrill of building and growing and the profits that come from those activities. We blue-collar entrepreneurs thrive on the thrill of the hunt and not necessarily the taste of the meat we are going to eat after the hunt is over. So, typically it's not until the need arises for the sale, that entrepreneurs give any significant amount of thought and effort into the details of the exit strategy and that is a sure fire way to end up being broke and disappointed with yourself after the sale is concluded.

Shark Tank

If you ever watch Shark Tank and listen closely to the comments of the sharks, especially when they don't do a deal, you should listen to the reasons why. A lot of times, especially Kevin who is focused very strategically on the money in the deal, if you hear him say that the only way for him to recapture his investment or make any money on the deal is if someone is willing to acquire the company after he invests and then he quickly, in his head, calculates the size of the deal that would need to happen in order for him to double or triple his investment. Many times the reason he doesn't invest in a company is because the company owner, the entrepreneur, has no definite exit plan that will have enough money in it for Kevin to cash out at any significant gain.

This is very atypical thinking of the entrepreneur, he thinks about the short term profits of the company and how he can either invest or spend that money but very little thought, at least at first, goes into strategically positioning the business for a buyout.

In my own case my last company was purchased by a strategic buyer, more on the types of buyers in a later section, and had prepared myself for that sale and that exit almost accidentally. I did the work that I knew was going to grow my company and automate the processes, but mainly I did that to reduce my own workload and make my life easier. It turns out that those reasons are very similar to how you would structure any business for sale. Growing the business and preparing it for sale are not mutually exclusive activities. They can both achieve the same goal. A potential buyer at the $10 million level is going to want systems in place and operational, with ROI calculated and documented. So you will certainly need to have a system for systematizing your business processes. Buyer's are going to want something pointed out to them that sets your business apart from all the others they are considering for purchase, which in a large way is why you must know how to market your business. This is different from marketing your products and services, though some of the same principles apply.

You Want Out

The buyer is going to want to know where the new growth is going to come from and that the reasons you are getting out match well with why they want to get in. So the reason I wanted to get out was because I had been doing it for 16 years and grew tired of it, fit in just perfectly with their desire to position my business as a new value added service to their clients. They understood the real reason I wanted out, which turned out to be very common and they understood that reason. But if I had told them I was getting out to go run another similar company then that would have raised red flags to them and might not have fit in with what they wanted to accomplish.

I had always planned this business to be my long-term retirement. I envisioned from day 1 that I would have a number of options on how I wanted to get out of the business and cash out of this investment. I just never had the details outlined or thought out exactly when that was going to be and exactly what those options were, since there are really so many different ways to get out of a business.

So the planning of the exit on the front end needs to be more detailed than just a general idea in order to achieve an 8 figure exit. The exit planning process will closely resemble a marketing plan, well, that's because instead of selling a product you are selling your business so we go through some of the same steps as we covered in the marketing section of this book.

Timing

Timing can also be a critical factor in selling the business and the best time of course to sell is when the business is on an upswing. I have a client right now that owns a hydraulic repair business. They repair hydraulic motors and hoses and sell fittings to the farmers and oilfield businesses here locally. It is a family business with 2 couples running the company for 30 plus years. About 6 years ago one of the husbands died and the other husband took on more responsibilities. Well, 6 months ago that husband died too and now it is being run by two 72 year old widows who are in very poor health. Actually, I should say it is just barely hanging on, not really being run by anyone, just limping along and barely surviving. I just mentioned that even with a losing venture you can still make a profit. But, in order to make that happen you have to have the marketing and systematization already in place. Now unfortunately, these two ladies are contemplating selling the business because they really don't have the strength or desire to continue to run the company and they want to move away from the business and closer to their families for the remaining years of their life. Their husbands did not have a well thought out exit plan either, so they really don't have many options.

So, having an exit plan that is brought on by tragedy is a terrible time to have to make an exit plan. There will be no way for these two widows to get any substantial value out of the business other than maybe the value of the physical assets because they are in dire need to sell the company just to cover their daily living expenses. Currently the plan is very limited in options on how they can exit. The possibility of a large payday is just about non-existent and they are having to make some very tough realizations that what they thought they had as a thriving business would have been much more valuable to them had they planned to exit before any one of the 4 partners had died. But this plan would have had to start being planned many years prior, actually a convenient time would have been when they purchased any life insurance and began to think about succession of their personal assets since the business really is a personal asset.

If you have not engineered your exit plan into your overall business plan, now that the business is growing quickly, it is time to plan an exit strategy and prepare the business for the type of exit you consider to be most appropriate for you. The best time to actually sell the business is when you can show the track of increasing revenue as opposed to decline revenue over a 36 month period, which is the typical timeframe looked at during a buyers due diligence and especially the last 12 to 24 months.

You Need To Get Personal

You must get personal. You must begin planning your exit strategy with a clear written definition of your personal financial and non-financial goals. In the investment community there is a term called the 4% rule. It describes in detail, which I won't get in to here, that if you invest conservatively that by living off the interest only of your investments you can safely live off of an amount equal to 4% of the principle amount. So, if you sell your business and clear $10 million after taxes and closing costs then you can have a yearly budget of $400,000 without digging into the principle, theoretically lasting you eternally. With this thought process, you should begin to ask yourself two very important questions. The first questions is – "Can I live off of $400, 000 per year or some multiple of that amount?" $200,000 per year means a $5 million sale or $100,000 per year means a $2.5 million sale. The second question, and probably the more important of the two is "Is my business worth anywhere near that amount?"

What's The Business Worth

Know how your business is valued and what it is worth at every point in time – Understanding how your business interest will be valued when you sell it, will help you gain an understanding of the variables over which you have control and how to drive them to attain your expected value threshold. For example: I mentioned that the last 3 years preceding the year I sold my business had been very, very phenomenal. I added over $1.2 million to the vale of my business by putting in place direct marketing systems as well as got my business running on autopilot by systematizing the other 5 areas of my business. By getting my sales, marketing, leadership, management, production and money systems in place and operating at a much higher level than ever before I was able to substantially raise the value of my company to any potential buyer. When I coupled the better systematization with the tremendous successes over the last 36 months, I had positioned my business for the peak sales price.

How Much Do You Need

So often the first question entrepreneurs ask when it comes time to sell is: "What is my business worth?" when really the question should be "How much do I need to live like I want to?" This is a very personal number and when you are armed with that number then it becomes simply a plan to make your personal number match the value of the business and find a way to get someone to pay you that amount for it. Not only is the number important but the timing is important as well. Do you need all of the money right away? With the right securities in place you can give more buyers better options to purchase your business and you help them to finance it. Many times businesses are not purchased as a cash sale, there typically is some type of note carried by the seller for some period of time. This of course induces more risk into the deal but the risk can certainly be mitigated with the right legal structures in place. I have also seen that many times deals fall apart because seller try to get every penny worth of value out of their business and they don't focus enough on the bigger goal which was to make sure that the sale of this business matched their long term goals. They really need to make sure that the sale meets their long-term goals rather than the amount primarily.

This is the time when you need to consult the right members of your team, but you need to ask the right questions. That is really the point of this entire set of 5 phases. The buying and selling of businesses, the organic and exponential growth of your business is not something you can do alone, you must have a team. But you absolutely need to know strategically how all of these pieces fit together so you can at least speak intelligently and ask the right questions. You don't need to know how to word the documents so you are legally covered, but you sure as hell need to know that there are many options as to how to finance a deal so that both the buyer and seller get what they want. Your team may know the answers but if you don't ask the right questions they won't think to advise you of every possible way to get these types of deals done. So this exit preparation includes that you as the seller educate yourself on the possible strategic ways to get out while meeting your goals and then you can consult your team for the details and tactics to make this strategy become a reality.

Exit planning requires the participation of multiple business advisors. Savvy entrepreneurs engage the support of experienced dealmakers as their personal coach or project mentor to ensure their exit plan stays on course.

Your sale team will include:
1. The business broker or investment banker for screening potential buyers best suited for your exit need.
2. The Transaction accountants/auditors for audit of financials and addressing financial due diligence issues potential buyers may raise.
3. The Tax accountants for deal structuring and tax due diligence issues.

4. The Valuation advisor for independent value determination and assessment.
5. The legal team for legal representations, warranties and reviews.
6. The financial advisor for retirement and estate planning.
7. The deal advisor for general coaching and support system for the business owner. Now, unknown to many people this person or group of people help the business owner to really understand and double check what they need to do and how they need to do it even though you as a business owner is still responsible for the ultimate decision just like Walter explained earlier on. Yes, you do not need to know the technical nitty-gritty of what needs to be done, but you need to educate yourself on those essential matters on things that are critical to the selling or the exit. Your deal coach may actually be your own in house person that goes about gathering that information and making those things accessible to you while you are focusing on the day-to-day operations of your business.

Planning for and putting this team together in preparation for your exit is the most important and critical thing that you can do to ensure that you extract the most for your effort. The sale team is the mastermind for every successful exit: it makes or breaks the entire process.

<u>Never, ever, ever attempt a sale of your company by yourself!</u>

Your sale team members will have earned their weight in gold after you see just how much they have assisted you in extracting the most money for your business.

I would like to caution you here. Do not put your business up for sale until you are truly ready to sell! You must have had a plan because the goal is to extract the most value and receive the most cash upfront. Moving forward without a plan is foolish and a surefire way to be taken advantage of by a more experienced and savvy buyer. Get yourself a detailed plan.

I mentioned many different roles of the buy team and want to make sure that you understand that these are simply roles that need to be filled and not necessarily separate people for each one of these roles. My team was built through my normal business operations. I already had a CPA and attorney I that had prior experience with acquisitions. I mentioned earlier that building a business and positioning it for sale are not necessarily mutually exclusive and this is a perfect example of that. So you'll already have some of these relationships previously established through your normal business operations.

With a knowledgeable sale team in place their job primary job is to stage and position your business to command the maximum value. You will have aligned yourself with the group of people whose interests are literally aligned with yours even though you have been paying them in the ordinary course of your business relationships with them, by getting them involved in the sales process that will have a very rare opportunity to participate in the monetization of your business vision.

While you may not always be thinking about that with every thing you do you are primarily serving dual purposes by growing your business properly and documented well, having a good marking system in place you are doing both of those things at the same time. So don't think of them as two separate actions to take because the both to servicing purpose.

Over and over I think that there are quite a few things I would do differently. One thing would be to have experience from the other side of the table, because it is so vitally important to first understand why someone would want to buy your company in order to get the maximum amount of money for it. So once you truly understand what the buyer wants from the deal and then being able to structure and to position your company to suit the buyers needs adds immense value to the transaction as well as sets you apart from all other businesses he may be considering buying. In essence this can become your USP for selling your entire company. This act alone potentially adds multiples to the value of your company.

So let's take a look at what the buyers of my business had planned for what was going to happen after they bought my company. Fist off they definitely had a detailed Acquisition Priorities and Criteria list and it showed how to lay out the priorities of the acquisition and what the potential business criteria are that would allow you as the buyer to meet those goals and priorities.

So let me lay out what their plans and priorities were.

1. They wanted to double the size of their client list. So one of their criteria must have been to have identical types of clients with minimal overlap of their current clients and roughly the same number of clients as they currently have. We both had roughly the same type and number of clients.

2. Sell a product or service that would compliment their current products and services. Their services dealt with hydraulic and mechanical equipment and my company dealt with electronic equipment, so this was a fit as well.

3. A growing company so they could take advantage of an upturn in the company to add to the other criteria.

4. Fully operation business systems making sure that there was duplication of job functions at both companies. Now this may sound counterintuitive that they would look for a business that had a duplication of internal business processes, but I will show you very soon why they wanted that.

So with these 4 criteria here is how this is executed without violating my confidentiality agreement, here are the hypothetical rough numbers of what's going on.

Their first step was to add $10 million in sales to their business, but it cost them $10 million to acquire me. Over time they will eventually recuperate that cost, so in essence it is break even for the first 3 to 5 years. Then there will be profit in the deal just for the acquisition.

Secondly they took the services of my company and sold those services to their clients and the reason criteria 1 was to make sure we both had roughly the same number and types of clients was so with this one move they doubled the sales of my company. So now a $10 million transaction turned into a $20 million, but they didn't stop there.

Next they took their products and services, now they had multiple products and services they offered and I only had 1, but conservatively they just doubled their customer base and conservatively added yet another $10 million to their sales. So $10 million becomes $30 million in value. But they didn't stop there.

Next they reduced expenses of my business substantially by getting rid of any duplication of costs. Combined we now had 2 locations in one major area, so they closed that location and thereby reduced payroll, rent, utilities, etc.. And sold off duplicate assets like some of the internal business equipment as well as any other production equipment that was duplicated between the businesses. Then there was no reason to have duplicate personnel for HR, Accounting and even some sales staff. They shaved off those expenses and created more profit. Then, they took advantage of my growth with my new marketing system since it was unique and added value to their clients as well. So now, over time, with all these changes they added yet another multiple of the price they paid me for my company to their transaction value. This meant that a $10 million deal turned into $40 million deal within 3 to 5 years very easily. All because they had a plan with criteria set on the front end of the deal and essentially grew their investment by 400%. This is a perfect example of paying full retail value for a company and making it a great deal because you are prepared to take full advantage of all available opportunities.

Had I realized up front what the guys on the other side of the table were going to do, I could have done it myself by acquiring other more complimentary businesses as I grew my company over the 16 years since I founded it.

Given my experience I see the methods really clearly from the strategic buyer's viewpoint and so since I see it more clearly and the fact that typically strategic buyers pay more for a company than financial buyers, I could have taken action earlier on in the growth of my company to groom it even better for a strategic buyer. In order to make it large enough for the sale of this size that I eventually closed, I could've done it faster had I groomed the business to be sold to a strategic buyer from the very onset.

Not that it wouldn't have been of interest to a financial buyer, but since I had a relationship with my industry and clients and since that is where the largest pool of strategic buyers are coming from, it was really easy to understand their needs, what they saw in my company and helped make the transaction much smoother. I also think censure getting involved in this kind of a system that goes from the very basics of marketing all the way through selling the business for 8+ figures, that you should certainly consider all the different types of exits and not just focus on the ones that you are come with. Personally, I was more comfortable with people that I spoke the same language with in my industry. But, had someone expressed interest in my business that was not a strategic buyer or even one of my competitors I still would have pursued that type of exit because even though I wasn't familiar with that type of exit strategy, even though I would be uncomfortable speaking to someone outside of my industry. Into those who are unfamiliar with any of the strategies what a great opportunity to be able to learn all of them before you have to unlearn any other exit strategies.

This is a really good case to have a business broker or an experienced team with you to know what are the right questions to ask and the timing of these questions. And it's important to note that the timing of the due diligence of the buyer is very crucial. For obvious reasons, most of it needs to be done before the you agree to a "standstill agreement" that might prohibits you from negotiating with any other prospects. It is also done before you spend even more time in negotiations, money for advisory fees and before bringing in the key employees into the negotiations.

Owners of private companies are frequently being contacted today by potential buyers asking if they want to sell their company.

1. Private equity groups are sitting on a stockpile of investor cash that needs to be put to work

2. Some "brokers" are hungry for listings and are calling owners pretending to have a buyer interested in "their" company

3. Larger companies are looking to replace shrinking margins through acquiring their smaller, but in most instances, more profitable, competitors or complimentary businesses.

4. Many of the buyer prospects are "bottom fishers", or are just looking for bargains, regardless of the industry and the owner is just one on a list of several hundred calls the buyer will be making.

But there are some very credible buyers in the market place today. Some are spreading the word that they are pro-active in acquisitions and are talking with many seller prospects, while others are targeting only a few specific companies they want to buy and are quietly entering into serious negotiations. Unfortunately, the prospects do not come clearly labeled, which leaves you, the seller, with the daunting task of finding out just how serious the buyer is in buying your company and whether the prospect has the financial resources to get through the transaction. So it is in your best interest to ask probing questions before you get too far into the negotiation process.

Here is what you, as the owner, need to find out about the prospective buyer on the initial contact:
- Is the person making the contact with you the principal or a representative of the principal (a broker)?
- Has the buyer done his homework on your industry or is he already a member of this industry?
- Does the buyer know the challenges of owning your type company?
- Has the buyer made any acquisitions in your industry?
- Does the buyer have a track record of those acquisitions?

Once you have these questions out of the way, you can feel a little more comfortable in spending more time learning about what the buyer has in mind. You'll of course have many more questions later but this should get you moving forward with a little more peace of mind. Also keep in mind that some of these questions may seem sensitive or embarrassing and cause awkward situations so it might be appropriate to use your attorney instead of causing a disruption in the much needed friendly relationship at this time between the buyer and the seller.

Here are some of the things you will need to know about the buyer's financial ability:
- Where is the buyer getting its money?

- Is the buyer borrowing the purchase price from the bank? If so, is the seller's deferred payment subordinated to any senior bank borrowings?
- What is the bank's role in approving the acquisition?
- What is the collateral for the deferred payment?
- Are there any pending lawsuits that, if settled against the buyer, may impair the buyer's ability to make your installment payments?
- Is the buyer making the purchase through a "thinly capitalized" corporation and not guaranteeing its debts?
- What's the buyer's track record on previous purchases?

A good indicator of how well a buyer keeps his promises and performs during the negotiations and after closing are the comments from sellers who sold their company to the buyer. The seller's team should ask the buyer for references, and make inquiries to the buyer about prior acquisitions. Again, it's in this area that the experienced deal manager can provide a good source of information on how well the buyer performs.

Here are some of the questions to ask in checking the buyer's track record:
- How many deals has the buyer completed?
- Were the sellers satisfied with the buyer's performance?
- Did the sellers receive all of their deferred purchase price? If not, Why?
- How long did it take the buyer to consummate the transaction?
- What conditions is the buyer placing on the deal?

Although the price and terms are very important aspects of every deal, the conditions which must be met in order to receive the money is just as important. Many of the conditions are found in the purchase agreement, but some may be oral and relate to how the company is run during any period you may be guaranteeing the continuation of the accounts.

Most buyers don't prepare the purchase agreement until they finish their due diligence. Since you need to know the conditions that will be in the contract before the buyer starts its due diligence, you should ask for a sample agreement, or at a minimum should find out the conditions the buyer will require for this deal.

A word of caution about the sample purchase contract: in reviewing the sample contract, your advisors should make sure that the sample contract is compatible with your type of transaction. If it isn't, some of the provisions will not apply or will be different. Also, there may be conditions to your deal that may not be in the sample contract.

Here are some of the important things to know about the conditions to the deal:

- Is the deal structured as a stock or asset transaction? (The answer to this question may have a dramatic tax consequence to you.) Typically Sellers want a stock sale and buyers want an asset sale when looking strictly at tax advantages but there will be may more factors affecting they type of transaction you will want.
- What is the approval process?
- Does the buyer require a guarantee of the accounts? If so . . . What's the duration of the guarantee?
- Will the buyer allow the seller to replace lost accounts with new accounts?
- Will the buyer allow the new accounts to increase the purchase price?
- Is the seller protected in the event an account leaves because the buyer did not properly service the account?

- How is the company run during the guarantee period?
- Which of the seller's personnel will be retained?
- Will the operating name be changed?
- What is the seller's involvement during the transition?
- What is the expiration period of the representations and warranties in the purchase contract?
- Is the deal signed and closed simultaneously? If not, what's the seller's liability in the period between signing and closing?
- When and how is the sale announced to the employees and general public?
- Will a portion of the selling price be allocated to a covenant not to compete? If so, how much? (The answer to this question could have a significant tax impact on the seller. The amount of the impact, positive or negative, depends on whether the seller is organized as an S or C corporation.)
- Are the buyer's operating philosophies compatible with those of the seller?

This is very important if there is an account retention condition to the seller getting all its money after closing. The customers need to stay happy after the sale, or they may leave. Therefore in order for the deal to be successful and the accounts be happy after closing, the buyer and seller must be compatible. They must share common philosophies on providing service to the customers, career paths, and benefits for the employees. Much of the compatibility checking can be done through negotiating meetings with all the seller's and buyer's team members present. However, the seller spending one on one time with the buyer principal in a non-business setting affords the opportunity to find out things that would not ordinarily be learned from the structured meetings.

A good setting for this "get together" is a quiet restaurant or a golf game. Part of my transaction occurred while we ate crawfish in a really relaxed atmosphere. You can both be more relaxed and will often use this as a way to resolve difficult issues that may have surfaced in the formal meetings. It's also a good setting for discussing the buyer's conditions that may not be appropriate to handle in the formal purchase agreement.

A Word of Caution:

The preceding is not intended as an all-inclusive list of due diligence items. It's merely a presentation of some of the your concerns in checking out the buyer prospect. Each deal is different and the degree to which a buyer should be examined varies. This is another reason you MUST have a well put together deal team well before you consider selling your company.

Once all this has been done you have met the right buyer and they have responded positively to all the potential issues you have raised that means the deal is closed. But, what do you need to immediately after the transaction closes.
Once the ownership has been transferred and your sale team has ensured that your total entitlement from the sale is assured, you are now free to look to the future beyond the business!

This next phase is more emotional and psychologically draining than most people plan for. With this program, you won't fall into that category.

Specifically, you want to:
1. Protect the value you have extracted.
2. Minimize tax liabilities and exposures.
3. Creative low-risk, lifetime and passive income opportunities.
4. Establish structures to protect family and future heirs.
5. Consider options for staying active, nimble and relevant professionally, not necessarily for the money.
6. Consider how you can build a legacy
7. Evaluate opportunities for a second coming.

Chapter 8

Freedom Day

A Far Off Dream

Sitting here right now listening to me, the day may seem like a far off dream in the distance. A day when you wake up naturally, no alarm clock screaming at you to start your day. You feel your body coming to life naturally as a great peace sets into you when you remember, you realize, that this is not merely a weekend or a day playing hooky from the office. You blissfully recall that you're not just on vacation really since it won't be just one or two weeks before you have to go back to work. This is long term, it can be forever if you want it to last that long. The hustle and bustle of the business is gone and you now choose to live your life with liberation. You've put in the time and effort and broken the chains of exchanging you hours for dollars. Now your life is all about the choice, the freedom to live how you want to. And you know you got to experience this first day of the next phase in your life because you chose to live a short time focusing, building, transforming and working like most men won't so that you could live the rest of your life like other men can't. That's your Freedom Day!

For many years my young son would come to me and want to play. Hey Dad you wanna' come play Mortal Kombat with me, hey Dad you wanna' come swimming in the pool with me, hey Dad you wanna' come play nerf gun wars with me? Well, for me, that answer used to always be NO. It had to be no. I was running a multi-million dollar company with 40 employees and locations in 6 states, there was simply no extra time to stop every evening and take the time to play. Didn't my 10 year old son Evan understand that I was doing this for him too. This was at some point going to create a freedom for him too. Well, today, on my freedom day, I was able to say YES. That is what the liberation really was to me, being able to say yes every time was what I toiled for all of those years. I now had the time for playing, not only with him doing mortal kombat video games and taking an hour to just go and jump in the pool any time we felt like it or grabbing his nerf guns out of his closet and running around the house shooting each other and maybe breaking a lamp or knocking over a picture or two. This was what I wanted to accomplish. This may not be your freedom day, but what will your freedom day look like? What will your freedom day feel like? When will your freedom day happen?

Well if you follow the path we have set up for you in the last few chapters, now you are at least on the way to that destination. In chapter four, you have taken the time and implemented your foundational marketing pieces and started getting great ROI. Your advanced marketing pieces are building higher and higher levels of trust with your clients. Chapter five gave you a system to document your many business systems and a fully developed employee training program. These two skills will be crucial tools that you take to the negotiation table in chapter six where you learned the basics of acquisitions and then honed your skills as you added financing and integration to your repertoire. As you built your empire the day draws closer in chapter seven where you were lead through the strategies and tactics to be able to sell your business and cash out at a level you never could have reached had you stayed on your previous path, simply hoping that someday you were going to reach the eight-figure level. Now you are here, the business is sold and your freedom day is upon you.

When we are talking about freedom, when we are talking about liberation there are two major parts to it. We have been discussing throughout this entire program about the first thing, money. There are certain finances that are required to achieve this freedom. The second thing is time. Time is a precious resource and both time and money are finite resources, but time is the most finite of all resources. There is no way to get more time, there is no way to speed up or slow it down, there is no way to earn more by doing more. And I think that's really one of the key lessons of this program is that you certainly can take your business and building and grow it and you can certainly sell it with only doing a few of the things that we've covered in this program.

But, what we have really managed to accomplish what you will really be able to accomplish now that we've shown you this path is that you can take the time that you would have spent growing, building and cashing out of your business and instead have that time to do the things that are true to your heart.

So let's take a look at this process of liberating you from your business in a way that suits your future lifestyle.

Change of command ceremony

One of the first things that's going to go on is what I witnessed many times in the Navy called a change of command ceremony. On board a US aircraft carrier I was stationed on for 4 years, the USS Carl Vinson (CVN-70) I had this experience twice in 6 years and each time it was a little bit different.

The first time it happened the outgoing Captain of the ship was a tyrant. Very strict in his discipline, very demanding of his officers, time for liberty (that's what the navy calls getting off of work) was frequently minimal and overall a very disliked man. This was the only high level officer I ever saw that had 2 armed sideboys. (That's a military term for 2 Marine bodyguards) that kept the Captain safe from his own crew he was so despised by his entire crew. So this first change of command was all by the book with officers and crew lined up in perfect rank and file, all there because it was ordered so by this man that was so truly hated. As soon as it was over there was simply a low almost whispered quite amongst the men as we ate cake (because we were ordered to) and then as quickly as we could and the ceremony was officially over, we got the hell out of there and sighed a great relief as the old captain left and the new one stepped in.

The second change of command was quite different, because this second captain was almost a mirror opposite of the first and truly loved, thoroughly equally respected by his crew. We worked hard for him, but he showed a lot of appreciation and gratitude towards his officers and crew and was well liked and ran a very highly decorated ship. (Yep, ships actually get medals, but instead of being pinned on your chest like they do on soldiers and sailors uniforms, they paint them on the top mast to show its' level of combat readiness). So this change of command ceremony came after 3 years of his command and the ceremony was joyous, dignitaries attended (Former President Clinton was there) lots of Admirals from around the fleet. The entire crew attended and they had dancing and a meal served voluntarily by the crew. We had a great time, though it was bittersweet because we knew he was leaving.

So my change of command ceremony was more joyous and bittersweet. There was a slideshow of the years gone past, a celebration with joyous laughter and reminiscing. The new CEO stepped in and I handed over my keys to the building, ceremoniously of course, I still had a few months of an employment agreement to fulfill. And then it was over and I was to take on my new role.

Demoted CEO

Then reality set in. There I sat in the smaller corner office in a remote area of the building, no secretary, no office with a view, no authority – Just a demoted CEO, no longer wanted or needed. After building this company from nothing more than a mere idea in my head to a $10 million payday, it was really an anticlimactic sendoff. I wasn't really leaving, the ceremonial handing over of the keys was just that, ceremonious, I really still had a set of keys and I was still going to go into the office for the next 6 months to handle the transition over of the company to the new CEO. After going 90 miles an hour for 16 years to build this company, there was a bit of relief that the workload was going to be shared and then finally disappear, but what took a long time to let go of was that feeling of responsibility for performance. I was there for 6 months, day to day, with the new guy and got to see mistakes being made but powerless to step in, I was there only to advise. I would wince when I saw some of those decisions being made, but hey, this was his chance to reign so he'll have to face the music with these decisions. In spite of knowing that I could let go because it wasn't my company any more, it was very tough to let go and see someone else sit in my office at my desk and run my company.

Transaction types

The type of transaction is going to play a huge role in what you do after the sale as well as the size of the transaction. In a $10 million plus size of sale, likely you have enough to never have to work again, even with a very conservative investment strategy. With this size of sale you'll have the full freedom to decide whether or not you want to follow the serial entrepreneur path or you are ready to become fully retired and take on the role I refer to as the Business Founder. This is someone who is going to go into full retirement and take the time off to enjoy a slower pace with their family. But there is another pathway I referred to that I call the serial entrepreneur. In this decision to be a serial entrepreneur or a business founder is steered heavily by the type of transaction.

- Cash Sale
- Earnout
- Consulting Hybrid

Cash sale

If you got one big check then your mind it totally at ease. This type of transaction is a fairly clean break. Now all you need to do is to consult a financial planner specializing in distribution of wealth. Remember this, the guy you've been using to accumulate your money may not necessarily be the best person to handle this new phase of your money, spending it! Get professional help and explore many options, but get a team behind you just like you did for the buying and selling of your companies. This is supremely important to make sure it is done correctly the first time. You won't likely get another shot at earning 8 figures again, this is an irreplaceable amount of money so get involved with someone with experience handling money at that level and in this phase of your life.

Earnout

This is a payment structure where you are paid with the earnings of the existing company. Long term and short term - You still have some involvement at the company and you'll need to keep on eye on the KSI's monthly to keep yourself aware of what's going on – keep apprise of the current health of the company with the systems put into place in Phase II. You should plan at least monthly in person meetings, if not more often at first to go over the business financials and all other KSI's. Your financial future rests on the shoulders of someone else so you'll want to make sure they are doing a better job than you could have done alone.

Monitoring company performance - this is when you are going to thank the gods that you did a great job with your key strategic indicators.

Consult for your old business (Consulting Hybrid)

Many entrepreneurs think that when they sell the business they are simply going to get out and have no more dealings with the company. Or, that they will stay in and manage the business at some level. There is also the idea that the only time money will exchange hands during the sale of a business is at the closing, but that is not necessarily true. This consulting hybrid I am referring to is another way to earn money and only be minimally involved with the operations of your company. Who better to be familiar with the business operations from your previous company than its previous CEO. So when your old company is in need of help than you are in a position to serve as a consultant and get paid well for it. Act as a paid consultant to your old company as a highly skilled and very uniquely qualified consultant that can demand high fees for their help with the business. This can be just as or even more financially lucrative than the sale of the business itself. This type of arrangement can certainly be documented in the closing articles especially if the business is being paid through an earn-out. It is in the best interest of the outgoing CEO to be at the top of the list when the business needs help.

Your Second Coming

Something I do want to mention about getting back involved is having the second coming. In my own case personally I know that I am a serial entrepreneur and I will get back involved within this industry but not necessarily in the same type of business. I also want to emphasize that not only will you need a buy team and a sell team, but you will also need a team to support you after the sale of the business. You will need financial advice from a qualified wealth advisor that specializes in distribution versus accumulation of wealth. Many of my investments are targeted for very conservative growth with maximum security of the principle. I have always made sure I live well below my means and that really continues today too. I bought a couple of toys to play around with but nothing extravagant. My wife, myself and now my 11 year old son love the water so we got a few small water toys and a place to go and enjoy them on a lake no too far from here. We spent the summer last year scuba diving in Grand Cayman and it was truly freeing to be able to spend the entire summer with my wife and son and not working at all.

I wanted to protect that lifestyle so the tax liabilities and exposures have been addressed by my tax attorney and an asset protection program involving different corporate structures for different assets and insurances. I am not going to get into the details but suffice to say that you will need an advisor for this area to make sure you cover your assets well.

Staying active and nimble professionally has been my biggest challenge to balance. When you have been performing at a really high level for so many years it is difficult to slow down and relax while at the same time keeping your mind sharp and relevant in business. So what I have found to work best for me is lots and lots of reading and consulting with other entrepreneurs. The reading keeps me up on current trends as well as growing educationally and the hours consulting helps to keep me abreast of the industry and challenges others are facing. This program is a perfect example of keeping relevant and nimble and staying involved at a high level while not compromising this opportunity to enjoy this other path, this other journey of freedom.

When I began this this book, this chapter was designed to give business owners an example of how it feels to experience their freedom day from their business. And though it tends to be at the end of this program, the psychological aspects of selling your business is really one of the first things that you should think about when preparing to exit your business. The reasons you want out are truly the most important part of this entire program. So we do this phase an injustice by putting it at the end of the program. The "why" of why you want to get out of business, the reasons for getting out are so personal and are so varied there is no way to go over all of them. So if your true passion lies somewhere else you can make this size the transaction, the timing of the transaction, the purchasing of other businesses for exponential growth and then the selling of your own business fit with all of the options we've shown to meet your own personal goals.

Are you ready to take the next logical step? Schedule your contractor market assessment. So you can identify the prospects that are 600 X more likely to turn into a new customer…and it's FREE too!
Simply go to www. MEERScore.com/freeoffer and fill out the application for a 45 minute phone call with Mike Layton.

As a special bonus, this includes an additional FREE strategy session to get your customized plan for exponential growth with Walter Bergeron.

Chapter 9

Follow In Someone Else's Footsteps

Easier Than You Think

This process is not as hard as you think it is. Sure I just gave you over 200 pages of actions to take, but just as any long journey starts with the first step so does the path to an eight-figure payday. The physical steps to take mean you'll need to sit at your desk and write some sales letters and develop some marketing on your computer. You'll need to make a few phone calls and set up a few meetings. You'll need to have lunches with your colleagues and discuss strategies with other business owners. You may need to have a tough conversation or two during the negotiations and stand your ground when you make a decision. This is what this process is all about, but doesn't this resemble what you're doing now as the leader of your business. At some point in your career haven't you already done many of these activities? Of course you have, well then you'll just do them again but the topics and the goal will be to buy and sell businesses. This is new information to you and new strategies but it isn't rocket surgery or brain science.

The Right Questions

You of course will have a team, actually multiple teams working with you and for you to complete these actions and you will rely on their expertise. You simply have to know the right questions to go to your team with, then they will give you the answers and guide you through the strategic and tactical processes to complete whatever needs to be completed. You will need to know some specialized strategies so you can guide your team and allow them to help you do a little course correction but you are the captain and you steer the ship so you'll need to know where you are going and they'll help you get there.

Work Both Sides First

Having the experience as a buyer first will make you a much more powerful seller. Being able to have experienced what it takes to get to the point of making an offer and following

---

through with an acquisition will prepare you in ways you could never imagine when it comes time to sell your company. This is an area where if you simply rely on your team to have all of the experience they may guide you in ways that may not work to your maximum benefit so you'll need to have sat on the other side of the table to get the best deal when you sell.

Leverage Up

Your business must be going in the right direction before you start the acquisition process. If your growth is negative then the leverage you get with an acquisition will just point your negative growth downward even faster. So the first step is to get the business growing organically and then apply the leverage of acquisitions to speed up the process of growth.

Get Started Now

It takes time to sell a business for 8 figures so you'll need to get the process started now. Many business owners get discouraged when it comes time to sell their business when they find out that it takes months and sometimes even years to get everything done. What they don't realize is that growth and preparation to sell the business are not mutually exclusive activities. Simultaneously growing and preparing the business to sell while performing acquisitions compresses this time frame to get to the sale substantially faster.

Get A Guide

Big game hunters rarely just go hunting in an area all alone without first getting a guide to show them where to go, how to find the game and then how to make the final kill shot. So, just as a hunter would first find someone to help them with their hunt, so should you get someone to guide you in your hunt of big game to buy your company. Your guide should know the area well and have accomplished what it is you want to accomplish. You certainly can do it on your own but beware that you are playing with big game and it's likely that you'll get eaten alive without knowing what you are doing.

This Is What You Need To Do Now

If you've read to this point in the book you are undoubtedly motivated and driven to get to your own liberated lifestyle. The next logical and savvy step to take is to get yourself your own customized plan to exponentially grow your business and then sell it for 8 figures. So go to www.WalterBergeron.com/strategyfree to set up a time to speak one on one with someone that can give you that plan.

Once I have your complete contact information, you'll get an email from my office with an application and a way for us to set up a time to talk. Our initial call will be between 45 and 60 minutes. This is our strategy session and where we really begin working to figure out exactly what you want ...and how to make it happen. I get paid $2500 for this strategy session time after time so I know it's worth every second we talk. Of course you're getting it at no charge.

I'll painstakingly review your goals, your offers, and so forth...and I'll deliver a plan to bring in money immediately and grow your business long term, plus let's not forget about the possibility of selling it for $10 million dollars. You get the full $2500.00 value from our conversation and it won't cost you one red cent!

This opportunity is extremely limited because of the intense one-on-one time needed in order to provide you with results. Therefore, it is physically impossible for me to work with more than a handful of people. Also, you should realize there's a very large demand for personal one-on-one help from me, and what I'm offering to you is unprecedented. So with that said, know that the window of opportunity won't be open long.

Are you ready to take the next logical step? Schedule your contractor market assessment. So you can identify the prospects that are 600 X more likely to turn into a new customer…and it's FREE too!
Simply go to www. MEERScore.com/freeoffer and fill out the application for a 45 minute phone call with Mike Layton.

As a special bonus, this includes an additional FREE strategy session to get your customized plan for exponential growth with Walter Bergeron.